FLOWER FARM ✿ SAMPLER

18 FLORAL BLOCKS & 7 FANCIFUL QUILTS

SHELLEY CAVANNA

C&T PUBLISHING
Another Maker Inspired!

Text copyright © 2025 by Shelley Cavanna

Photography and artwork copyright © 2025 by C&T Publishing, Inc.

Publisher: Amy Barrett-Daffin

Creative Director: Gailen Runge

Senior Editor: Roxane Cerda

Editor: Madison Moore

Technical Editor: Debbie Rodgers

Cover/Book Designer: April Mostek

Production Coordinator: Zinnia Heinzmann

Illustrator: Shelley Cavanna, Linda Johnson

Photography Coordinator: Rachel Ackley

Front cover photography by Melissa Gayle

Lifestyle Photography by Melissa Gayle, unless otherwise noted

Subject Photography by C&T Publishing, unless otherwise noted

Published by C&T Publishing, Inc., P.O. Box 1456, Lafayette, CA 94549

Library of Congress Cataloging-in-Publication Data

Names: Cavanna, Shelley, author.

Title: Flower farm sampler : 18 floral blocks & 7 fanciful quilts / Shelley Cavanna.

Description: Lafayette, CA : C&T Publishing, [2025] | Summary: "Inspired by spring and summertime flowers, Shelley Cavanna shares eighteen blocks and seven quilt designs that bloom and shine. The Flower Farm Sampler quilt incorporates the different block designs spanning 4″ to 24″ in a fresh sampler-quilt layout. Combine the blocks from the sampler quilt to create a variety of other stunning projects"-- Provided by publisher.

Identifiers: LCCN 2024040247 | ISBN 9781644035351 (trade paperback) | ISBN 9781644035368 (ebook)

Subjects: LCSH: Quilting--Patterns.

Classification: LCC TT835 .C3977 2025 | DDC 746.46/041--dc23/eng/20240920

LC record available at https://lccn.loc.gov/2024040247

Printed in China

10 9 8 7 6 5 4 3 2 1

Dedication

For my Granny. For sharing her joy in crafts of all shapes and sizes since the very beginning.

Acknowledgments

While being a designer is oftentimes a solitary job, the transformation of an idea to a book takes a village. Words can't express my gratitude for my quilty family in helping bring this book to life.

To my guys—Rob, Aiden, and Jamie. Thank you for the unending supply of hugs and caffeinated beverages. I couldn't have done this without you, and your support means the world to me. I love you to the moon and beyond!

To Cara of Sew Colarado Quilting, not only for your superb quilting skills, but also for your amazing ability to always pick the perfect quilting designs.

To C, K, and L—my mastermind kindred spirits and the best hype squad a gal could ask for; I love you three!

To Jessica, my incredible creative director at Benartex, for helping me dream up these beautiful fabric collections! And to my fabric family at Benartex for providing all the fabric for the quilts in this book.

To Melissa, of Melissa Gayle Photography, for all of these gorgeous, flower-filled photos. And to the Ranch at Stoney Creek for providing the perfect background to bring my imaginary Flower Farm to life!

To my C&T publishing family—working with you has been a dream come true and I can't wait to start our next project together!

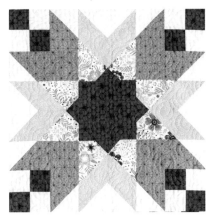

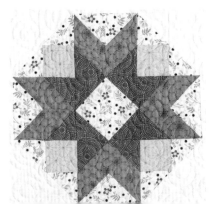

CONTENTS

INTRODUCTION

I've always dreamed of living on a flower farm, of looking out my window to find that I'm surrounded by a bevy of beautiful flowers and a cacophony of riotous color and texture.

In reality, I was born with the sad talent of killing just about every plant I bring home. My family calls me the green acre undertaker. Maybe that explains my obsession with bold floral prints and beautiful blooms recreated in fabric. Fabric flowers have the magical ability to live on for eternity, in spite of my rotten gardening skills.

If you don't know this about me already, the only thing I love more than flowers are sampler quilts. I love that each new block is a new adventure…and a short term sewing commitment. I love that making samplers gives dozens of chances to play with simple shapes and put them together in creative and interesting ways. And I'm all for that thrill of almost-instant gratification that finishing a few small blocks in the space of a few hours brings!

So, I am very excited to be sharing *The Flower Farm Sampler* quilt with you! I've set this book up so that you can work through it in small segments, all at once, or block-of-the-month style if you choose. I've created it with the hope that you'll frequently get to spend a few joyful hours getting lost in your fabric garden and coming out the other side with some lovely, pieced blocks.

Happy sewing! ~ *Shelley*

How To Use This Book

This book contains eighteen floral-inspired blocks ranging from 4″ to 24″. *The Flower Farm Sampler* quilt uses all 18 blocks in a fresh and modern take on a traditional sampler.

In addition to the sampler quilt, you'll find six bonus projects that showcase just a few blocks at a time in more traditional quilt layouts.

THE QUILT BLOCKS

In general, I suggest working from the largest 24″ blocks to the smallest 4″ blocks when piecing the sampler. Especially if you are a confident quilter or making your project from a scrappy stash, start with the largest blocks (Blocks 1–3) and work your way through chronologically, saving the smallest blocks for last.

But, if you are a beginning quilter, we suggest starting with the 8″ blocks (Blocks 10–14). Beginning with the smaller blocks turns this sampler into a skill-builder project, giving you the chance to practice individual techniques on a smaller scale before moving on to the more complex blocks that combine a variety of different shapes and techniques. After completing the 8″ blocks, move on to the 16″ blocks and then the 24″ blocks.

Whichever order you choose, work on the smallest blocks (Blocks 15–18) last. These blocks are really meant to function as *blender blocks*. They help to balance out the colors and prints that you use in the larger blocks. We've provided fabric requirements for the exact prints we've used in these tiny blocks, but feel free to mix in as many of your own prints or repurposed scraps as you'd like!

THE FABRICS

The fabrics used in the pictured Flower Farm quilt are mainly prints from my Secret Garden fabric collection with Benartex Fabrics, along with prints from my other fabric collections and a few basic blender prints.

The Flower Farm Sampler (page 14) has tips and tricks for selecting your own fabrics, along with a link to a downloadable swatch page where you can attach snippets of your fabrics and keep track of your prints.

THE MATERIAL LISTS

Each quilt and project has its own materials list, so you'll know exactly how much of each print you'll need. We've placed the two smallest projects at the end of the book, the *Climbing Roses Mini Quilt* (page 78) and *Among the Wildflowers Table Runner* (page 84), knowing that if you've worked your way through several of the other projects, chances are that you have some leftover scraps and triangle trimmings ready to be used.

THE CUTTING INSTRUCTIONS

To make the cutting lists short and sweet, we've used icons to indicate which type of shape you need to cut. Be sure to pay close attention while cutting because some squares might need to be subcut diagonally in half or in quarters. The four icons we'll be using are:

□	▭	◩	⊠
Square	Rectangle	Square cut in half diagonally to yield 2 triangles	Square cut into quarters diagonally to yield 4 triangles

In the cutting instructions, each piece is assigned a letter. The piecing instructions and assembly diagrams then refer to each piece by these letters, making it easy to see exactly where each piece is used in each block.

SAMPLE CUTTING TABLE

Fabric		Yardage and Cutting List
	Cosmos Teal FABRIC 6	Yardage: 1 fat quarter Cut: A: 36—2½″ × 2½″ □
	Nightshade Grass FABRIC 10	Yardage: 1 fat eighth Cut: B: 3—4½″ × 4½″ □
	Sprigs Navy FABRIC 18	Yardage: 1 fat quarter Cut: C: 12—4½″ × 2½″ ▭ D: 12—2½″ × 2½″ □

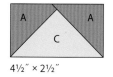

4½″ × 2½″

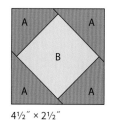

4½″ × 2½″

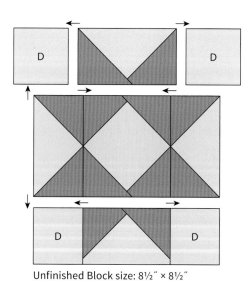

Unfinished Block size: 8½″ × 8½″

STITCH-AND-FLIP TUTORIALS

We've provided a separate tutorials chapter for some of the frequently used stitch-and-flip shapes we'll be making throughout the book. See Stitch-and-Flip Basics (page 10).

Use that chapter as a quick reference guide for making commonly used shapes, but be sure to look at the instructions and illustrations for each block to see the exact pieces to use and the angle/placement of the sewing lines.

Best Practices

FLOWER FARM STITCHING RESOURCES!

For a full list of my preferred tools, video tutorials of my favorite tips and techniques—from pre-washing and starching fabric to the various stitch-and-flip piecing techniques—block coloring pages and more, visit my website (see Let's Connect, page 88).

This book assumes that you have a basic knowledge of quiltmaking terms and techniques. None of the projects in this book require any specialty rulers, paper or foundation piecing templates, or inset or Y-seams. You'll be able to piece the majority of the projects in this book using only squares and rectangles. The few blocks that have triangular components are pieced larger than required, and then trimmed down to the perfect size.

STARCHING AND PRE-WASHING

Starching and pre-washing fabric is a bit of a contentious topic among quilters. I find the greatest quilting success by skipping the pre-wash and heavily starching my fabric before cutting. In my own practice, I find that starched fabric gives me some extra stability while piecing and yields really crisp, accurately finished blocks.

That being said, you should do what gives you the best result in your own quilting practice. Be sure, however, to pre-treat all the fabric within a quilt with the same preparations.

PRESSING MATTERS!

How to press seams is another hot-button topic for quilters, so my honest advice to you is press your blocks in whatever way gives you the best results!

In my own quilting practice, I use nesting seams whenever possible and find that pressing my seams to one side or the other helps me match my points most accurately.

You'll find my suggestions for directional seam pressing indicated by arrows in your assembly diagrams, *but they are just suggestions*. Some blocks will stubbornly refuse to listen to instruction, and some blocks might work better for you if their seams are pressed open. Not all seams will nest—and that is perfectly fine. Please press in whatever manner gives you the best result!

And, you will find some blocks that suggest pressing components open to reduce bulk! Typically (although not always) these are elements that are buried within the block, rather than along the edges of the block. Wherever they live, if you're pressing your seams open, I recommend backstitching at the beginning and end of those seams to eliminate the chances of the seam unraveling after you've joined it to its neighbors.

I also strongly suggest investing in a felted wool pressing mat. The mat absorbs the heat from the iron and reflects it into the back side of the block so that you are essentially pressing from both sides at the same time. The result: superbly flat blocks without a lot of fuss!

GENTLY!!

Be gentle as you press! Start by pressing the seam with the block closed to set the seam. Then, open the seams with your fingertips. Finally, press using an up-and-down motion with the iron. To avoid block or seam distortion, try to avoid moving the fabric around with the iron.

STITCH-AND-FLIP BASICS

Whenever possible, the blocks in this book use stitch-and-flip techniques to make complex, geometric shapes quickly and easily, using very few individual fabric components. To make a stitch-and-flip shape, you first mark your stitching line on the wrong side of a square or rectangle. Then, you place it right sides together with another square or rectangle, stitch on the marked line, trim away the excess fabric, and press!

And the best part? You're sewing angular blocks *without any triangles or stretchy bias edges!* If you can stitch on a marked line, then you can make any of these shapes!

These tutorials are meant to be a quick reference guide for making commonly used shapes, so they don't include letter labels or dimensions. Be sure to look at the instructions and illustrations for each block to see the exact pieces to use, the angle/placement of the sewing lines, the specific pressing instructions, and the unit dimensions.

MARKERS MATTER!

It is so very important to use a chalk pencil or water-soluble pen to mark your stitching lines. By using a temporary marking tool, any lines that bleed through to the front of your quilt are easily removed.

I do not recommend using thermo-sensitive gel pens to mark your fabric, as the ink may look like it has "disappeared", but the ink remains in your fabric and can actually reappear.

Stitch-and-Flip Corners

The most basic stitch-and-flip unit is the stitch-and-flip corner! It's a very simple and efficient way to embed a triangle in a quilt block without using a triangular piece of fabric.

1. Mark a diagonal line, from corner to corner, on the wrong side of a square; this is the stitching line. Paying careful attention to the direction of the line, lay the marked square, right sides together, on top of the unit you're adding the corner to—called the *base piece*—taking the time to carefully line up your corners.

2. Sew on the marked line. Then, trim the excess corner fabric ¼″ away from the stitched line.

3. Press as directed.

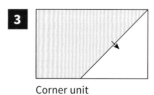

Corner unit

STITCH-AND-FLIP FLYING GEESE

Flying Geese units are just rectangles with stitch-and-flip corners added to each end. The stitch-and-flip corners overlap by ¼″, so that when the unit is joined with its neighbor, the apex of the triangle just kisses the seam.

1. Mark a diagonal line, from corner to corner, on the wrong side of 2 squares. Paying careful attention to the direction of the line, lay the first marked square, right sides together, on top of the base rectangle. It doesn't matter whether you start at the left end or the right end; in the end, your finished block will appear the same either way. Stitch, trim, and press, repeating Steps 2–3 in Stitch-and-Flip Corners (left).

2. Repeat Step 1 to stitch, trim, and press the second marked square to the opposite end of the base rectangle, making sure that the marked line is placed as shown.

STITCH-AND-FLIP SQUARE-IN-A-SQUARES

Another variation of the stitch-and-flip block is the square-in-a-square unit, which has stitch-and-flip corners added to all 4 corners of a base square.

1. Mark a diagonal line, from corner to corner, on the wrong side of 4 squares. Pin 2 marked squares, right sides together, to opposite corners of the base piece as shown.

2. Stitch, trim, and press, repeating Steps 2–3 in Stitch-and-Flip Corners (left).

3. Repeat Steps 1–2 to pin, sew, trim, and press the remaining 2 marked squares.

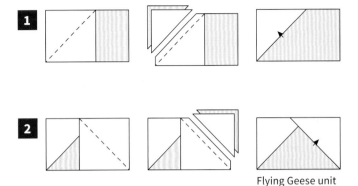

Flying Geese unit

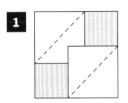

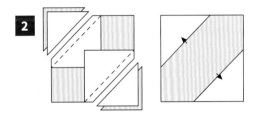

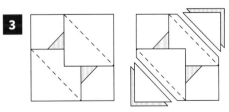
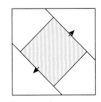

Square-in-a-square unit

STITCH-AND-FLIP SQUARE-IN-A-RECTANGLE

Some blocks use square-in-a-rectangle units in place of square-in-a-square units that would otherwise need additional fabric added at the top or bottom edges to make them taller.

These square-in-a-rectangle units use 4 corner squares (2 are larger and 2 are smaller) against a rectangular base. The 2 larger squares are sewn to the upper corners of the rectangle and create a seam allowance that is intentionally greater than ¼″ to build in that extra height.

To make this unit, repeat Steps 1–3 in Stitch-and-Flip Square-in-a-Squares (page 11). Pin 1 small and 1 large square opposite each other as shown. Be sure to flip the larger square out of the way when stitching the smaller square opposite it.

Stitch-and-Flip Rectangles

You can also join rectangles together using stitch-and-flip seams to make a variety of leaning diamond units.

1. Pin a rectangle at a perpendicular angle on top of the base piece, as shown in the assembly diagram. Making sure that the corners of both rectangles are aligned, mark a diagonal line from the top left corner of the top rectangle to the bottom right corner of the bottom rectangle, as shown.

> ### USE YOUR CUTTING MAT!
> Try lining the rectangles up with the 45-degree line on your cutting mat to help you visualize the correct angle as you mark the seam-lines! To see this tip in action, visit my website (see Let's Connect, page 88).

2. Sew on the marked line. Trim the excess corner fabric ¼″ from the stitched line.

3. Press as directed, doing your best to keep the top and bottom edges of the unit in a straight line.

Square-in-a-square unit; ¼″ overlap

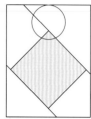

Square-in-a-rectangle unit; larger overlap

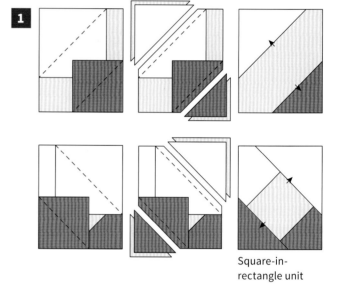

Square-in-rectangle unit

Rectangle unit

Two-at-a-Time Half-Square Triangles

Sometimes it's more practical to use a half-square triangle unit instead of a stitch-and-flip corner unit. My preferred method for making these units is to make them two-at-a-time using 2 squares!

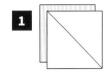 

1. Mark a diagonal line, from corner to corner, on the wrong side of 1 square. Pin it, right sides together, to the base piece, lining up all the corners.

2. Sew a scant ¼″ seam along *both sides* of the marked line.

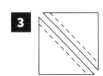 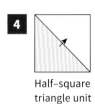

Half-square triangle unit

3. Cut the unit apart on the marked line to make 2 half-square triangle units.

4. Press the seams as directed, and then center and trim the unit down to size as directed in the block pattern.

Bonus Half-Square Triangles

With larger stitch-and-flip corners, you can repurpose the triangle trimmings into half-square triangle blocks. As you're stitching the square to the base piece, sew a second seam (on the corner segment you'll be trimming off) that is ½″ from the original stitched line. Then, when you trim off the excess fabric ¼″ from the first seam, you'll be trimming off a half-square triangle unit rather than 2 triangles!

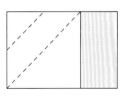 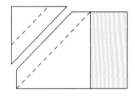

Results in stitch-and-flip corner rectangle and half-square triangle

Stitch-and-Flip Success

- **Practice first!** Practice new techniques with scraps first!

- **Mark lines carefully!** Use a water-soluble fabric pen, a chalk fabric pencil, or other *temporary* marking tool to mark stitching lines. This way, if the line accidentally bleeds through to the front of the block, it's easy to remove.

- **Try glue basting.** If you're having difficulty with the pieces wiggling around as you sew or you're frustrated with the extra bulk of sewing with pins—*and you don't have other plans for your triangle trimmings*—try glue basting! Use a water soluble glue stick to place a tiny dab of glue anywhere on the corner that you'll later trim off and discard. This will help the units stay securely in position as you sew.

THE FLOWER FARM SAMPLER

FINISHED QUILT: 80½″ × 100½″

Selecting Fabric

The fabrics used in the sample *Flower Farm* quilt are mainly prints from my Secret Garden fabric collection with Benartex Fabrics, along with a few prints from my other fabric collections and some basic blender prints. To see more on the fabrics, visit **CorasQuilts.com/fabric**

BACKGROUND FABRIC

For the background fabric, I used a variety of low-volume, white-on-white prints, mixed in with some more colorful small-scale prints that feature a white background. I love that this adds unexpected pops of color and loads of visual interest to catch your eye and draw it all around the quilt.

If you would prefer using a single background, however, you can use 5⅝ yards in place of Fabrics 20–24.

The Humble Quilt Sampler

FABRIC ALLOTMENT

I've provided very generous fabric requirements for this project to give you the flexibility to work in the style of a block-of-the-month if you choose! Expect to have leftover fabric from the sampler, knowing that you can use it for a scrappy companion quilt, to remake some of your favorite blocks for pillows, runners, or mini quilts, or to add to your stash!

I've calculated the yardage so that if you're working with fat eighths or fat quarters, you'll be able to cut the pieces for your block with at least a 1″ × width-of-fabric (WOF) margin. I've also built in an extra little bit of wiggle room to the overall yardage of the full quilt, so that you'll have a little bit of extra fabric in case you make a miscut or a piecing mistake.

FABRIC USAGE

We recommend that you always look through your scraps and cut pieces from any remaining strips left over from previous blocks before cutting a new strip. This project is meant to have a scrappy feel to it! But, I know that some quilters feel most comfortable sewing along with an exact fabric plan, so I've provided fabric requirements for the prints exactly as they're used in my version of the sampler.

EXTRA FABRIC

If you're following along with my exact fabric recommendations, and you make a mistake or run out of the print we've suggested, rest assured that there will be enough of another print in a similar color at the end to fix it. I recommend setting that block aside until you've finished piecing all the rest of the blocks, and then being creative in repurposing your leftovers.

If this "wait-and-see" philosophy sounds stressful, then you might want to purchase a fat quarter or two in each of the color families to have on hand, just in case.

A SCRAPPY SAMPLER

If you're a scrappy quilter, you can use this guide to help you pull a selection of scraps to make this quilt:

- 4 yards in Navy to be used as Fabrics 1–3 (includes ⅞ yard for binding)

- 1⅞ yards in Teal to be used as Fabrics 4–6

- ⅞ yard in Aqua to be used as Fabric 7

- 1¾ yards in Green to be used as Fabrics 8–10

- ⅜ yard in Yellow to be used as Fabric 11

- 2 yards in Plum to be used as Fabrics 12–13

- 2⅜ yards in Pink to be used as Fabrics 14–16

- 3½ yards in assorted prints with a white background to be used as Fabrics 17–19

- 5⅝ yards in low-volume background prints to be used as Fabrics 20–24

Flower Farm Fabric Requirements

This list includes all of the fabric needed to make the entire Flower Farm Sampler quilt as pictured if you piece the entire quilt from yardage.

Fabric requirements for each block can be found on the individual block pages, if you want to work on this quilt in the style of a block-of-the-month project. Yardage assumes 40″-wide fabric. Fat quarters assume 18″ × 20″. Fat eighths assume 9″ × 20″.

Additional Materials

- 89″ × 109″ rectangle of batting

- 7½ yards of 40″-wide fabric *or* 2½ yards of 110″-wide fabric for backing

NEED AN EASY WAY TO TRACK YOUR OWN SWATCHES?

For a free printable swatch sheet where you can attach snippets of your own fabrics, scan this QR code or go to **tinyurl.com/11598-patterns-download**

Assembling The Blocks

All measurements include ¼″ seam allowances. Check out How to Use this Book (page 6) and Best Practices (page 9) for general information for assembling each block.

For each block, the materials listed and the instructions yield the number of blocks needed for the *Flower Farm Sampler* quilt. If you are making a different quilt, refer to that project for the materials and the number of quilt blocks needed.

SAMPLER FABRIC REQUIREMENTS

Fabric		Fabric Amount
	FABRIC 1	2⅛ yards Nightshade Navy (includes ⅞ yard for binding)
	FABRIC 2	⅞ yard Secret Garden Navy
	FABRIC 3	1 yard Cosmos Navy
	FABRIC 4	⅜ yard Nightshade Teal
	FABRIC 5	⅝ yard Stitches Teal
	FABRIC 6	⅞ yard Cosmos Teal
	FABRIC 7	⅞ yard Filagree Aqua
	FABRIC 8	½ yard Stitches Moss
	FABRIC 9	½ yard Cosmos Leaves
	FABRIC 10	¾ yard Nightshade Grass
	FABRIC 11	⅜ yard Filagree Buttercup
	FABRIC 12	1 yard Nightshade Aubergine
	FABRIC 13	1 yard Cosmos Aubergine
	FABRIC 14	1½ yard Nightshade Sangria
	FABRIC 15	½ yard Cosmos Sangria
	FABRIC 16	⅜ yard Filagree Coral
	FABRIC 17	⅝ yard Secret Garden Vanilla
	FABRIC 18	1⅜ yards Sprigs Navy
	FABRIC 19	1½ yards Sprigs Sangria
	FABRIC 20	1¼ yards Macrame Cloud
	FABRIC 21	⅝ yard Filagree Cloud
	FABRIC 22	½ yard Queen Anne's Lace White
	FABRIC 23	½ yard Whisper Weave Too White
	FABRIC 24	2¾ yard Superior Solids White

BLOCK 1
WATER LILY

FINISHED BLOCK: 24″ × 24″

Materials & Cutting Instructions

Yields 2 blocks.

Fabrics		Yardage and Cutting List
	Nightshade Navy **FABRIC 1**	Yardage: ¾ yard Cut: A: 10—6½″ × 6½″ □ B: 8—6½″ × 3½″ ▭ C: 4—4″ × 4″ □ D: 8—3½″ × 3½″ □
	Secret Garden Navy **FABRIC 2**	Yardage: ½ yard Cut: E: 16—6½″ × 3½″ ▭
	Cosmos Teal **FABRIC 6**	Yardage: ⅜ yard Cut: F: 4—4″ × 4″ □ G: 16—3½″ × 3½″ □
	Sprigs Navy **FABRIC 18**	Yardage: ⅜ yard Cut: H: 24—3½″ × 3½″ □
	Filagree Cloud **FABRIC 21**	Yardage: ⅝ yard Cut: I: 8—6½″ × 3½″ ▭ J: 40—3½″ × 3½″ □

Piecing Instructions

Yields 2 blocks.

1. Sew together a D and a J square. Then, sew an I rectangle to the top edge. Repeat to make 8 units.

2. Paying careful attention to the angle of the seam, sew a J square to the top right corner of an E rectangle. See Stitch-and-Flip Corners (page 10). Trim and press. Repeat to make 8 units.

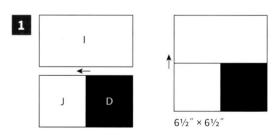

6½″ × 6½″

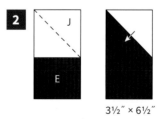

3½″ × 6½″

3. Sew 2 G and 2 J squares to an A square to make a square-in-a-square unit as shown. See Stitch-and-Flip Square-in-a-Squares (page 11). Repeat to make 8 units.

4. Paying careful attention to the angle of the seam, sew a J square to the top left corner of an E rectangle to make a mirror-image of the unit in Step 2. See Stitch-and-Flip Corners (page 10). Trim and press. Repeat to make 8 units.

5. Join 1 of each unit from Steps 2–4 into a row as shown. Repeat to make 8 units.

6. Use 4 pairs of C and F squares to make 8 half-square triangle units. See Two-at-a-Time Half-Square Triangles (page 13). Center and trim each unit to 3½″ × 3½″.

7. Sew 2 H squares to a B rectangle to make a flying geese unit. See Stitch-and-Flip Flying Geese (page 11). Repeat to make 8 units.

8. Sew 4 H squares to an A square to make a square-in-a-square unit. See Stitch-and-Flip Square-in-a-Squares (page 11). Repeat to make 2 units.

9. Arrange the units from Steps 6–8 in 3 rows as shown. Sew the units into rows, and then join the rows together. Repeat to make 2 units.

10. Arrange the units from Steps 1, 5, and 9 in 3 rows. Sew the units into rows and then join the rows. Repeat to make a second block.

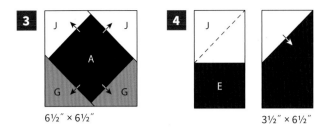

6½″ × 6½″   3½″ × 6½″

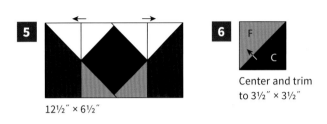

12½″ × 6½″   Center and trim to 3½″ × 3½″

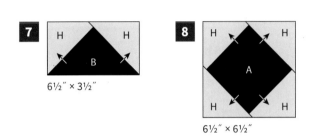

6½″ × 3½″   6½″ × 6½″

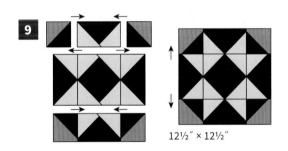

12½″ × 12½″

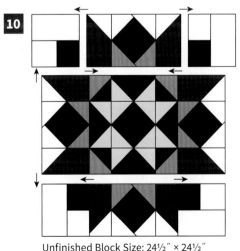

Unfinished Block Size: 24½″ × 24½″

Block 1: Water Lily

BLOCK 2
ENGLISH ROSE

FINISHED BLOCK: 24″ × 24″

Materials & Cutting Instructions

Yields 2 blocks.

Fabrics		Yardage and Cutting List
	Nightshade Aubergine FABRIC 12	Yardage: ½ yard Cut: A: 8—5¾″ × 5″ ▭ B: 2—5″ × 5″ ▢ C: 8—4″ × 4″ ▢
	Cosmos Aubergine FABRIC 13	Yardage: 1 fat quarter Cut: D: 8—5″ × 5″ ▢ E: 8—2¾″ × 2¾″ ▢
	Nightshade Sangria FABRIC 14	Yardage: ½ yard Cut: F: 16—8″ × 2¾″ ▭ G: 32—2¾″ × 2¾″ ▢
	Sprigs Sangria FABRIC 19	Yardage: 1 fat quarter Cut: H: 24—2¾″ × 2¾″ ▢
	Macrame Cloud FABRIC 20	Yardage: ¾ yard Cut: I: 8—8″ × 4½″ ▭ J: 8—4½″ × 4″ ▭ K: 32—3½″ × 3½″ ▢

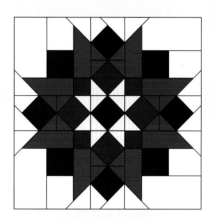

Piecing Instructions

Yields 2 blocks.

1. Sew together a C square and a J rectangle. Then, sew an I rectangle to the top edge. Repeat to make 8 units.

2. Arrange a unit from Step 1 with an E square and 2 F rectangles in 2 rows, as shown. Sew the units into rows, and then join the rows together. Press, spinning the seam between the 2 rows. Repeat to make 8 units.

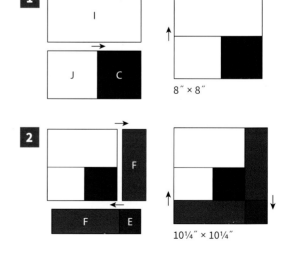

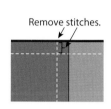
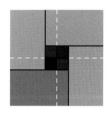
3. Sew 2 K squares to the upper right and lower left corners of a unit from Step 2 as shown. See Stitch-and-Flip Corners (page 10). Repeat for all 8 units.

4. Use an A rectangle with 2 G and 2 K squares to make a square-in-a-rectangle unit as shown. See Stitch-and-Flip Square-in-a-Rectangle (page 12). Repeat to make 8 units.

5. Use a D, 2 G, and 2 H squares to make a square-in-a-square unit as shown. See Stitch-and-Flip Square-in-a-Squares (page 11). Repeat to make 8 units.

6. Join a unit from Step 4 with a unit from Step 5. Press the seam open to reduce bulk. Repeat to make 8 units.

7. Use a B and 4 H squares to make a square-in-a-square unit. See Stitch-and-Flip Square-in-a-Squares (page 11). Repeat to make 2 units.

8. Arrange the units from Steps 3, 6, and 7 in 3 rows. Sew the units into rows, and then join the rows. Repeat to make a second block.

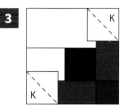
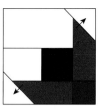

10¼″ × 10¼″

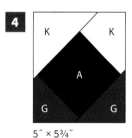

5″ × 5¾″

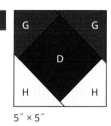

5″ × 5″

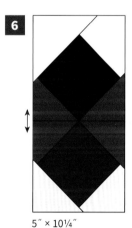

5″ × 10¼″

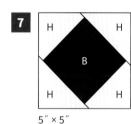

5″ × 5″

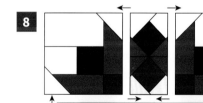
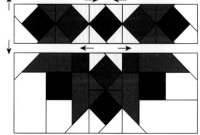

Unfinished Block Size: 24½″ × 24½″

BLOCK 3
LOVE IN A MIST

FINISHED BLOCK: 24″ × 24″

Materials & Cutting Instructions

Yields 2 blocks.

Fabrics		Yardage and Cutting List
	Cosmos Navy **FABRIC 3**	Yardage: ⅜ yard Cut: A: 2—7½″ × 7½″ ☐ B: 16—3″ × 3″ ☐ C: 16—2″ × 2″ ☐
	Stitches Teal **FABRIC 5**	Yardage: ½ yard Cut: D: 8—9″ × 4″ ▭ E: 8—5½″ × 4″ ▭
	Filagree Aqua **FABRIC 7**	Yardage: ½ yard Cut: F: 16—7½″ × 4″ ▭
	Secret Garden Vanilla **FABRIC 17**	Yardage: ⅜ yard Cut: G: 16—5½″ × 4″ ▭
	Superior Solids White **FABRIC 24**	Yardage: ¾ yard Cut: H: 32—4″ × 4″ ☐ I: 16—3″ × 3″ ☐

Piecing Instructions

Yields 2 blocks.

1. Arrange 2 B and 2 I squares in 2 rows, as shown. Sew the squares into rows, and then join the rows. Press, spinning the center seam (see Spinning Seams, page 21). Repeat to make 8 units.

2. Sew an E rectangle to the right edge of a unit from Step 1. Then, sew a D rectangle to the bottom edge. Repeat with all 8 units.

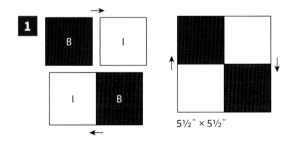

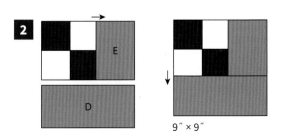

3. Sew 2 H squares to the upper right and lower left corners of a unit from Step 2 as shown. See Stitch-and-Flip Corners (page 10). Repeat with all 8 units.

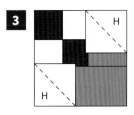 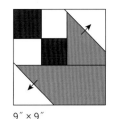
9″ × 9″

4. Paying careful attention to the orientation of the pieces and the angle of the stitching line, join F and G rectangles. See Stitch-and-Flip Rectangles (page 12). Repeat to make 8 units.

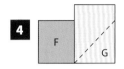 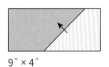
9″ × 4″

5. Sew an H square to the upper left corner of a unit from Step 4. See Stitch-and-Flip Corners (page 10). Then, sew a C square to the upper right corner as shown. Repeat with all 8 units.

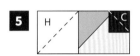 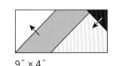
9″ × 4″

6. Paying careful attention to the orientation of the pieces and the angle of the stitching line, join F and G rectangles. See Stitch-and-Flip Rectangles (page 12). This unit is the mirror image of the units from Step 4. Repeat to make 8 units.

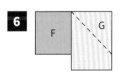 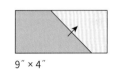
9″ × 4″

7. Sew an H square to the lower left corner of a unit from Step 6. See Stitch-and-Flip Corners (page 10). Then, sew a C square to the lower right corner as shown. Repeat with all 8 units.

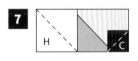 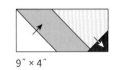
9″ × 4″

8. Join units from Steps 5 and 7 into pairs. Press the seam open to reduce bulk. Repeat to make 8 units.

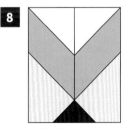
7½″ × 9″

9. Arrange the units from Steps 3 and 8 with an A square, in 3 rows as shown. Sew the units into rows, and then join the rows. Repeat to make a second block.

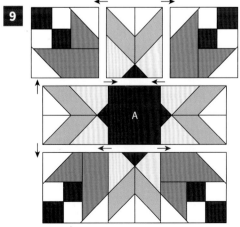
Unfinished Block Size: 24½″ × 24½″

Block 3: Love In A Mist

BLOCK 4
PRIMROSE

FINISHED BLOCK: 16″ × 16″

Materials & Cutting Instructions

Yields 2 blocks.

Fabrics		Yardage and Cutting List
	Nightshade Aubergine FABRIC 12	**Yardage:** 1 fat eighth **Cut:** A: 2—4″ × 4″ ☐ B: 8—2¼″ × 2¼″ ☐
	Cosmos Aubergine FABRIC 13	**Yardage:** 1 fat quarter **Cut:** C: 16—4″ × 4″ ☐
	Nightshade Sangria FABRIC 14	**Yardage:** 1 fat quarter **Cut:** D: 8—4″ × 2¼″ ▭ E: 24—2¼″ × 2¼″ ☐
	Sprigs Sangria FABRIC 19	**Yardage:** 1 fat eighth **Cut:** F: 24—2¼″ × 2¼″ ☐
	Macrame Cloud FABRIC 20	**Yardage:** ½ yard **Cut:** G: 8—7½″ × 1½″ ▭ H: 8—5″ × 3¼″ ▭ I: 8—3¼″ × 2¼″ ▭ J: 32—2¼″ × 2¼″ ☐

Piecing Instructions

Yields 2 blocks.

1. Sew together an I rectangle and a B square. Then, sew an H rectangle to the top edge. Repeat to make 8 units.

2. Use a C, an E, and 2 J squares to make a partial square-in-a-square unit as shown. See Stitch-and-Flip Square-in-a-Squares (page 11). Repeat to make 8 units.

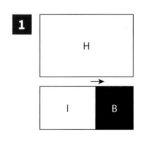

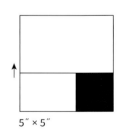

5″ × 5″

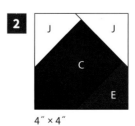

4″ × 4″

3. Use a C, an E, and 2 J squares to make a partial square-in-a-square unit that is the mirror image of the units from Step 2. See Stitch-and-Flip Square-in-a-Squares (page 11). Repeat to make 8 units.

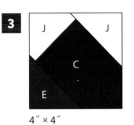

4″ × 4″

4. Join units from Steps 2 and 3 as shown, pressing the seam open to reduce bulk. Sew a G rectangle to the top edge. Repeat to make 8 units.

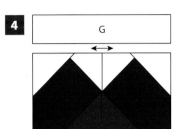
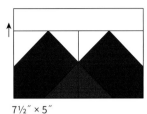

7½″ × 5″

5. Sew 2 F squares to a D rectangle to make a flying geese unit. See Stitch-and-Flip Flying Geese (page 11). Repeat to make 8 units.

6. Use 1 A and 4 F squares to make a square-in-a-square unit. See Stitch-and-Flip Square-in-a-Squares (page 11). Repeat to make 2 units.

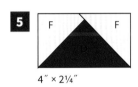

4″ × 2¼″

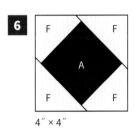

4″ × 4″

7. Arrange the units from Steps 5 and 6, along with E squares, in 2 rows as shown. Sew the units into rows, and then join the rows. Repeat to make 2 units.

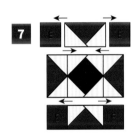

7½″ × 7½″

8. Arrange the units from Steps 1, 4, and 7 in 3 rows as shown. Sew the units into rows, and then join the rows. Repeat to make 2 blocks.

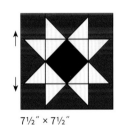

Unfinished Block Size: 16½″ × 16½″.

BLOCK 5
DAHLIA

FINISHED BLOCK: 16″ × 16″

Materials & Cutting Instructions

Yields 2 blocks.

Fabrics		Yardage and Cutting List
	Nightshade Teal FABRIC 4	Yardage: 1 fat quarter Cut: A: 24—3″ × 3″ □
	Cosmos Teal FABRIC 6	Yardage: 1 fat quarter Cut: B: 16—5½″ × 3″ ▭
	Stitches Moss FABRIC 8	Yardage: 1 fat eighth Cut: C: 8—3″ × 3″ □
	Sprigs in Navy FABRIC 18	Yardage: ½ yard Cut: D: 2—5½″ × 5½″ □ E: 32—3″ × 3″ □
	Superior Solids White FABRIC 24	Yardage: ⅜ yard Cut: F: 8—6″ × 3½″ ▭ G: 8—5½″ × 1″ ▭ H: 8—3½″ × 3″ ▭

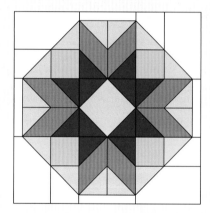

Piecing Instructions

Yields 2 blocks.

1. Sew an E square to the lower right corner of an F rectangle as shown. See Stitch-and-Flip Corners (page 10). Repeat to make 8 units.

2. Sew an E square to the lower right corner of an H rectangle. See Stitch-and-Flip Corners (page 10). Repeat to make 8 units.

3. Sew a C square to the right edge of a unit from Step 2. Then, sew a unit from Step 1 to the top edge. Repeat to make 8 units.

1

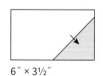
6″ × 3½″

2
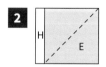

3½″ × 3″

3
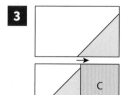
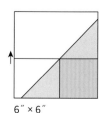
6″ × 6″

4. Paying careful attention to the angle of the seam, sew an E square to the upper left corner of a B rectangle. See Stitch-and-Flip Corners (page 10). Then, sew an A square to the lower right corner in the same way. Make 8 units.

5. Paying careful attention to the seam angle, sew an E square to the lower left corner of a B rectangle. See Stitch-and-Flip Corners (page 10). Then, sew an A square to the upper right corner in the same way. This unit is the mirror image of the units from Step 4. Repeat to make 8 units.

6. Join units from Steps 4 and 5 together as shown, pressing the seam open to reduce bulk. Then, sew a G rectangle to the top edge. Repeat to make 8 units.

7. Use a D and 4 A squares to make a square-in-a-square unit. See Stitch-and-Flip Square-in-a-Squares (page 11). Repeat to make 2 units.

8. Arrange units from Steps 3, 6, and 7 in 3 rows as shown. Sew the units into rows, and then join the rows together. Repeat to make a second block.

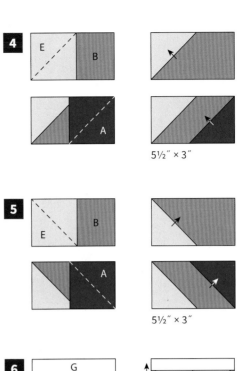

5½″ × 3″

5½″ × 3″

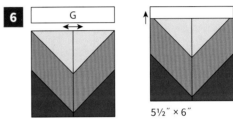

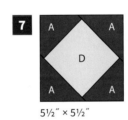

5½″ × 6″

5½″ × 5½″

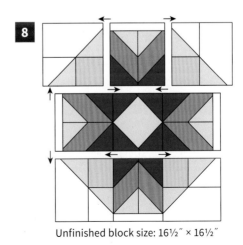

Unfinished block size: 16½″ × 16½″

BLOCK 6
GENTIAN

FINISHED BLOCK: 16″ × 16″

Materials & Cutting Instructions

Yields 2 blocks.

Fabrics		Yardage and Cutting List
	Nightshade Navy FABRIC 1	**Yardage:** 1 fat quarter **Cut:** A: 16—6½″ × 2½″
	Secret Garden Navy FABRIC 2	**Yardage:** 1 fat quarter **Cut:** B: 24—2½″ × 2½″
	Stitches Teal FABRIC 5	**Yardage:** 1 fat eighth **Cut:** C: 2—4½″ × 4½″
	Stitches Moss FABRIC 8	**Yardage:** 1 fat eighth **Cut:** D: 16—2½″ × 2½″
	Superior Solids White FABRIC 24	**Yardage:** ½ yard **Cut:** E: 16—4½″ × 2½″ F: 40—2½″ × 2½″

Piecing Instructions

Yields 2 blocks.

1. Arrange a B, 2 D, and 2 F squares, along with 2 E rectangles, in 3 rows as shown. Sew the pieces into rows, and then sew the rows together. Repeat to make 8 units.

2. Paying careful attention to the seam angle, sew an F square to the upper left corner and a B square to the lower right corner of an A rectangle as shown. See Stitch-and-Flip Corners (page 10). Make 8 units.

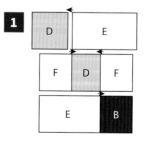
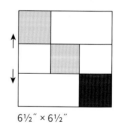

6½″ × 6½″

6½″ × 2½″

3. Paying careful attention to the seam angle, sew an F square to the lower left corner and a B square to the upper right corner of an A rectangle as shown. See Stitch-and-Flip Corners (page 10). This unit is the mirror image of the units from Step 2. Repeat to make 8 units.

6½″ × 2½″

4. Join units from Steps 2 and 3, pressing the seam open to reduce bulk. Repeat to make 8 units.

5. Use a C and 4 F squares to make a square-in-a-square unit. See Stitch-and-Flip Square-in-a-Squares (page 11). Repeat to make 2 units.

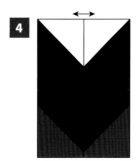

4½″ × 6½″

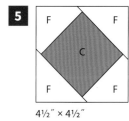

4½″ × 4½″

6. Arrange the units from Steps 1, 4, and 5 in 3 rows as shown. Sew the units into rows, and then join the rows together. Repeat to make a second block.

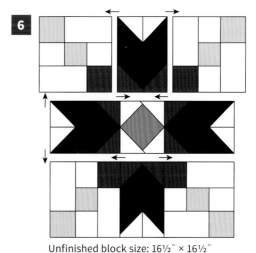

Unfinished block size: 16½″ × 16½″

BLOCK 7
ORCHIDS

FINISHED BLOCK: 16″ × 16″

Materials & Cutting Instructions

Yields 2 blocks.

Fabrics	Yardage and Cutting List
Cosmos Navy FABRIC 3	Yardage: ⅜ yard Cut: A: 2—4½″ × 4½″ B: 8—4½″ × 2½″ C: 4—3″ × 3″ D: 16—1½″ × 1½″
Cosmos Leaves FABRIC 9	Yardage: 1 fat quarter Cut: E: 8—4½″ × 2½″ F: 8—2½″ × 2½″
Nightshade Grass FABRIC 10	Yardage: 1 fat quarter Cut: G: 8—4½″ × 2½″ H: 8—2½″ × 2½″
Sprigs Sangria FABRIC 19	Yardage: 1 fat quarter Cut: I: 16—4½″ × 2½″ J: 8—2½″ × 2½″
Superior Solds White FABRIC 24	Yardage: ⅜ yard Cut: K: 8—4½″ × 2½″ L: 4—3″ × 3″ M: 32—2½″ × 2½″

Piecing Instructions

Yields 2 blocks.

1. Use 4 pairs of C and L squares to make 8 half-square triangle units (see Two-at-a-Time Half-Square Triangles, page 13). Center and trim each unit to 2½″ × 2½″.

2. Paying careful attention to the angle of the seam, sew an M square to the lower left corner of a B rectangle. See Stitch-and-Flip Corners (page 10). Repeat to make 8 units.

1

Center and trim to 2½″ × 2½″

2

4½″ × 2½″

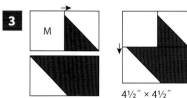
4½″ × 4½″

4½″ × 2½″

4½″ × 2½″

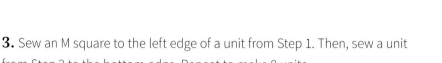
6½″ × 6½″

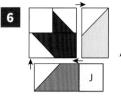
4½″ × 2½″

4½″ × 2½″

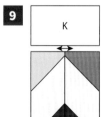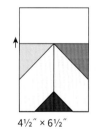
4½″ × 6½″

3. Sew an M square to the left edge of a unit from Step 1. Then, sew a unit from Step 2 to the bottom edge. Repeat to make 8 units.

4. Paying careful attention to the angle of the seam, sew an M square to the lower left corner of a G rectangle. See Stitch-and-Flip Corners (page 10). Repeat to make 8 units.

5. Paying careful attention to the angle of the seam, sew an M square to the upper left corner of an E rectangle. See Stitch-and-Flip Corners (page 10). Repeat to make 8 units.

6. Arrange units from Steps 3, 4, and 5, along with a J square, in 2 rows as shown. Sew the units into rows, and then join the rows together, spinning the center seam (see Spinning Seams, page 21). Repeat to make 8 units.

7. Paying careful attention to the seam angles, sew an H square to the lower left corner of an I rectangle. See Stitch-and-Flip Corners (page 10). Then, sew a D square to the upper right corner in the same way. Repeat to make 8 units.

8. Paying careful attention to the seam angles, sew an F square to the upper left corner of an I rectangle. See Stitch-and-Flip Corners (page 10). Then, sew a D square to the lower right corner in the same way. This unit should be the mirror image of the units from Step 7. Repeat to make 8 units.

9. Join units from Steps 7 and 8, pressing the seam open to reduce bulk. Then, sew a K rectangle to the top edge. Repeat to make 8 units.

10. Arrange the units from Steps 6 and 9 with an A square in 3 rows as shown. Sew the units into rows, and then join the rows together. Repeat to make a second block.

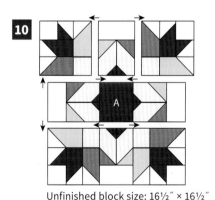
Unfinished block size: 16½″ × 16½″

BLOCK 8
SNAPDRAGONS

FINISHED BLOCK: 16″ × 16″

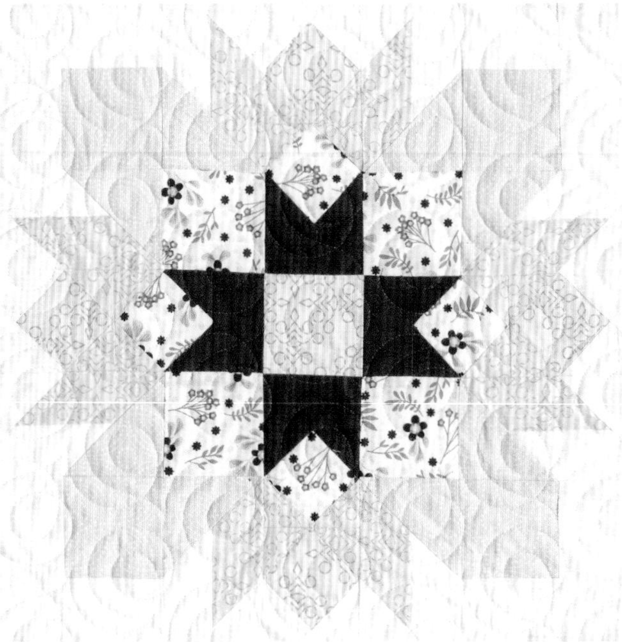

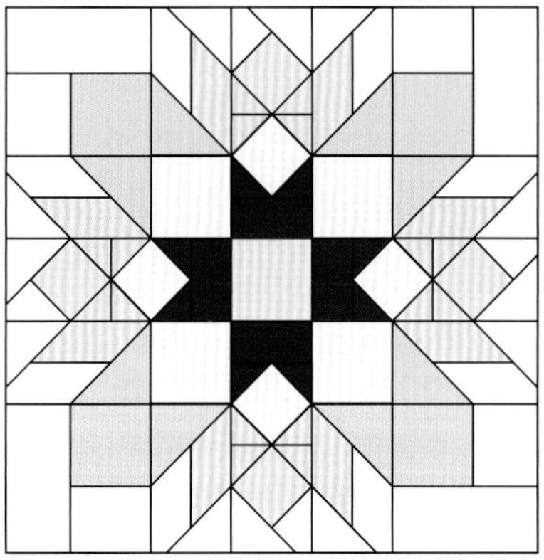

Materials & Cutting Instructions

Yields 2 blocks.

Fabrics	Yardage and Cutting List
Nightshade Grass FABRIC 10	**Yardage:** 1 fat quarter **Cut:** A: 24—3″ × 3″ □
Filagree Buttercup FABRIC 11	**Yardage:** 1 fat eighth **Cut:** B: 8—3½″ × 3″ ▭ C: 2—3″ × 3″ □
Cosmos Aubergine FABRIC 13	**Yardage:** 1 fat eighth **Cut:** D: 8—3″ × 1¾″ ▭ E: 16—1¾″ × 1¾″ □
Filagree Coral FABRIC 16	**Yardage:** 1 fat quarter **Cut:** F: 16—4¾″ × 1¾″ ▭ G: 32—1¾″ × 1¾″ □
Sprigs Sangria FABRIC 19	**Yardage:** 1 fat quarter **Cut:** H: 16—3″ × 3″ □
Queen Annes Lace White FABRIC 22	**Yardage:** ½ yard **Cut:** I: 8—4¾″ × 2¼″ ▭ J: 16—4¾″ × 1¾″ ▭ K: 8—3″ × 2¼″ ▭ L: 32—2¼″ × 2¼″ □

Piecing Instructions

Yields 2 blocks.

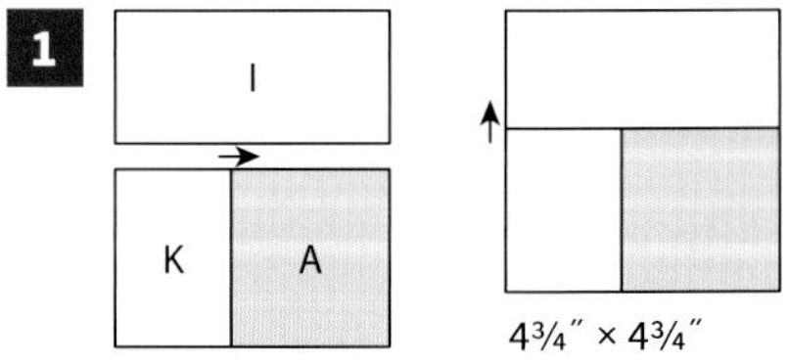

1. Sew together an A square and a K rectangle. Then, sew an I rectangle to the top edge. Repeat to make 8 units.

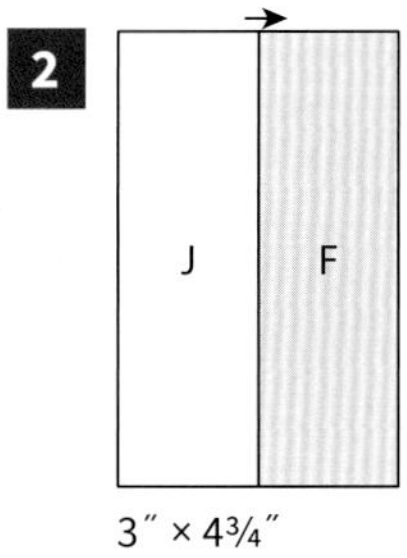

2. Sew together F and J rectangles. Repeat to make 16 units.

3. Paying careful attention to the orientation of the seam angles, sew an A square to the bottom left corner of a unit from Step 2. See Stitch-and-Flip Corners (page 10). Then, sew an L square to the upper right corner the same way. Repeat to make 8 units.

4. Paying careful attention to the unit orientation and seam angles, sew an A square to the bottom right corner of a unit from Step 2. See Stitch-and-Flip Corners (page 10). Then, sew an L square to the upper left corner the same way. This unit is the mirror image of the units from Step 3. Repeat to make 8 units.

5. Arrange units from Step 1, 3, and 4, along with an H square, in 2 rows as shown. Sew the units into rows, and then join the rows together. Press, spinning the center seam (see Spinning Seams, page 21). Repeat to make 8 units.

6. Use a B rectangle with 2 G and 2 L squares to make a square-in-a-rectangle unit. See Stitch-and-Flip Square-in-a-Rectangle (page 12). Repeat to make 8 units.

7. Use an H, 2 E, and 2 G squares to make a square-in-a-square unit. See Stitch-and-Flip Square-in-a-Squares (page 11). Repeat to make 8 units.

8. Join units from Steps 6 and 7, along with a D rectangle, in a column. Repeat to make 8 units.

9. Arrange units from Steps 5 and 8, along with a C square, in 3 rows as shown. Sew the units into rows, and then join the rows. Repeat to make a second block.

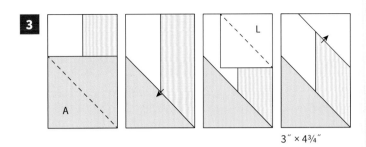

3″ × 4¾″

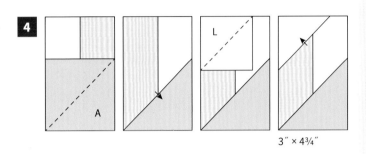

3″ × 4¾″

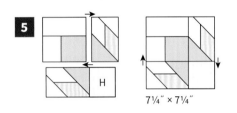

7¼″ × 7¼″

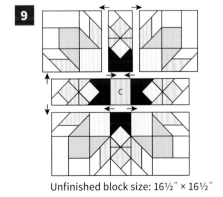

3 × 3½″

7 G G H E E 3″ × 3″

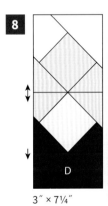

3″ × 7¼″

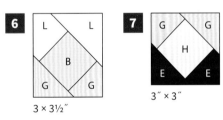

Unfinished block size: 16½″ × 16½″

Block 8: Snapdragons

BLOCK 9
PAPERWHITES

FINISHED BLOCK: 16″ × 16″

Materials & Cutting Instructions

Yields 2 blocks.

Fabrics		Yardage and Cutting List
	Secret Garden Navy FABRIC 2	Yardage: 1 fat eighth Cut: A: 4—5″ × 5″ □
	Cosmos Navy FABRIC 3	Yardage: 1 fat quarter Cut: B: 4—6″ × 6″ □
	Filagree Aqua FABRIC 7	Yardage: 1 fat quarter Cut: C: 4—6″ × 6″ □
	Nightshade Sangria FABRIC 14	Yardage: 1 fat eighth Cut: D: 8—3¼″ × 3¼″ □
	Whisper Weave Too White FABRIC 23	Yardage: ½ yard Cut: E: 12—5″ × 5″ □ F: 8—4½″ × 4½″ □

Piecing Instructions

Yields 2 blocks.

1. Use 4 pairs of B and C squares to make 8 half-square triangle units. See Two-at-a-Time Half-Square Triangles (page 13). Center and trim each unit to 5″ × 5″.

2. Mark a diagonal line on the wrong side of 8 E squares. Pin a marked E square right sides together to a half-square triangle unit from Step 1, making sure that the marked line runs opposite the center seam as shown.

Sew a scant ¼″ seam along both sides of the marked line, then carefully cut the unit in half along the line.

1

Center and trim to 5″ × 5″

2a E

2b

Press the seams towards E. This will yield 2 mirror-image units. Center and trim each unit to 4½″ × 4½″. Repeat with the remaining E squares and units from Step 1 to make 16 units (or 8 pairs).

3. Use 4 A and 4 E squares to make 8 half-square triangle units. See Two-at-a-Time Half-Square Triangles (page 13). Center and trim each unit to 4½″ × 4½″.

4. Paying careful attention to the seam angles, sew a D square to the lower right corner of a unit from Step 3. See Stitch-and-Flip Corners (page 10). Trim and press toward D. Repeat to make 8 units.

5. Paying careful attention to the orientation of each unit, arrange the units from Steps 2 and 4, along with an F square, in 2 rows as shown. Sew the units into rows, and then join the rows together. Press, spinning the center seam (see Spinning Seams, page 21). Repeat to make 8 units.

6. Arrange units from Step 5 in 2 rows as shown. Sew the units into rows, and then join the rows together. Press, spinning the center seam (see Spinning Seams, page 21). Repeat to make a second block.

Center and Trim
to 4½″ × 4½″

Center and trim
to 4½″ × 4½″

4½″ × 4½″

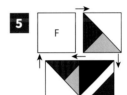

8½″ × 8½″

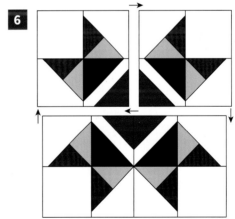

Unfinished block size: 16½″ × 16½″

BLOCK 10
STAR JASMINE

FINISHED BLOCK: 8″ × 8″

Materials & Cutting Instructions

Yields 3 blocks.

Fabrics		Yardage and Cutting List
	Nightshade Aubergine FABRIC 12	**Yardage:** 1 fat eighth **Cut:** A: 36—1¾″ × 1¾″ □
	Cosmos Sangria FABRIC 15	**Yardage:** 1 fat quarter **Cut:** B: 12—3¼″ × 3″ ▭ C: 12—1¾″ × 1¾″ □
	Filagree Coral FABRIC 16	**Yardage:** 1 fat eighth **Cut:** D: 3—3″ × 3″ □
	Sprigs Sangria FABRIC 19	**Yardage:** 1 fat quarter **Cut:** E: 12—3¼″ × 2″ ▭ F: 12—2″ × 1¾″ ▭ G: 24—2″ × 2″ □

Piecing Instructions

Yields 3 blocks.

1. Sew together a C square and an F rectangle. Then, sew an E rectangle to the top edge. Repeat to make 12 units.

2. Use a B rectangle with 2 A and 2 G squares to make a square-in-a-rectangle unit. See Stitch-and-Flip Square-in-a-Rectangle (page 12). Repeat to make 12 units.

3. Use 4 A squares and a D square to make a square-in-a-square unit. See Stitch-and-Flip Square-in-a-Squares (page 11). Repeat to make 3 units.

4. Arrange the units from Steps 1–3 in 3 rows as shown. Sew the units into rows, and then, join the rows together. Repeat to make 3 blocks.

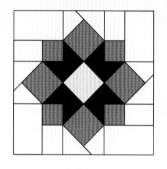

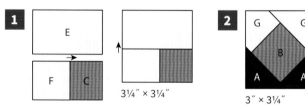

1

E

F C

3¼″ × 3¼″

2

G G

B

A A

3″ × 3¼″

3

A A

D

A A

3″ × 3″

4

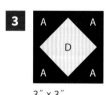

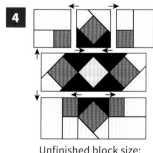

Unfinished block size: 8½″ × 8½″

BLOCK 11
MORNING GLORY
FINISHED BLOCK: 8″ × 8″

Materials & Cutting Instructions

Yields 3 blocks.

Fabrics		Yardage and Cutting List
	Nightshade Navy FABRIC 1	Yardage: 1 fat quarter Cut: A: 12—4½″ × 1¾″ B: 12—3¼″ × 1¾″
	Stitches Moss FABRIC 8	Yardage: 1 fat eighth Cut: C: 12—1¾″ × 1¾″
	Filagree Buttercup FABRIC 11	Yardage: 1 fat eighth Cut: D: 12—1¾″ × 1¾″
	Sprigs Navy FABRIC 18	Yardage: 1 fat quarter Cut: E: 12—3¼″ × 2″ F: 12—2″ × 1¾″ G: 24—1¾″ × 1¾″

Piecing Instructions

Yields 3 blocks.

1. Sew together a C square and an F rectangle. Then, sew an E rectangle to the top edge and press. Repeat to make 12 units.

2. Sew a B rectangle to the right edge of a unit from Step 1. Then, sew an A rectangle to the bottom edge. Repeat with all 12 units.

3. Sew G squares to the upper right and lower left corners of a unit from Step 2. See Stitch-and-Flip Corners (page 10). Sew a D square to the lower right corner the same way. Repeat with all 12 units.

4. Arrange the units from Step 3 into 2 rows as shown. Sew the units into rows, then join the rows and press, spinning the center seam (see Spinning Seams, page 21). Repeat to make 3 blocks.

1
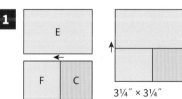
3¼″ × 3¼″

2
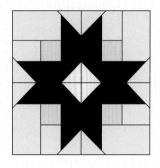
4½″ × 4½″

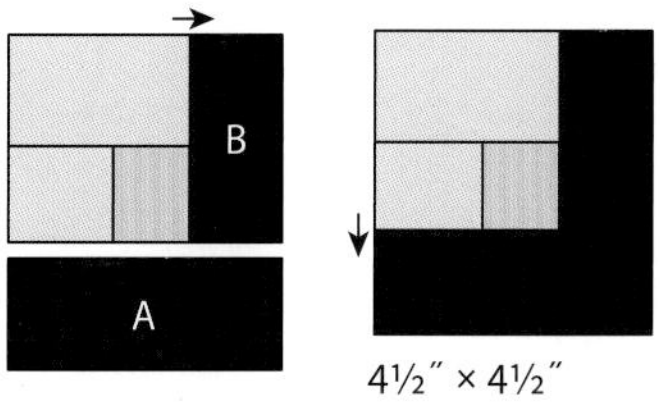

3

4½″ × 4½″

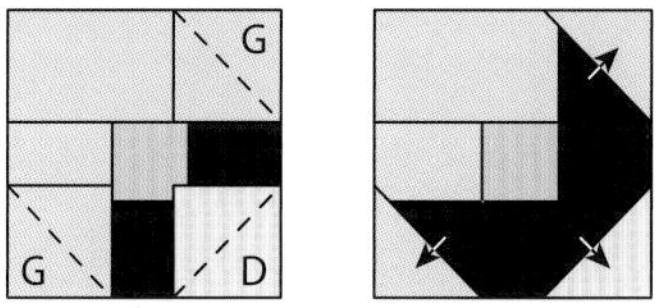

4
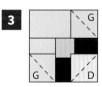

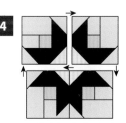
Unfinished Block Size:
8½″ × 8½″

BLOCK 12
LILY

FINISHED BLOCK: 8″ × 8″

Materials & Cutting Instructions

Yields 3 blocks.

Fabrics		Yardage and Cutting List
	Filagree Aqua **FABRIC 7**	Yardage: 1 fat eighth Cut: A: 24—2½″ × 2½″ ☐
	Nightshade Sangria **FABRIC 14**	Yardage: 1 fat eighth Cut: B: 3—2½″ × 2½″ ☐
	Secret Garden Vanilla **FABRIC 17**	Yardage: 1 fat quarter Cut: C: 12—3½″ × 1½″ ▭ D: 12—2½″ × 1½″ ▭ E: 24—1½″ × 1½″ ☐
	Superior Solids White **FABRIC 24**	Yardage: 1 fat eighth Cut: F: 12—2½″ × 1½″ ▭ G: 24—1½″ × 1½″ ☐

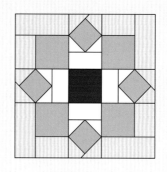

Piecing Instructions

Yields 3 blocks.

1. Sew together an A square and a D rectangle. Then, sew a C rectangle to the top edge. Make 12 units.

2. Use an A, 2 E, and 2 G squares to make a square-in-a-square unit. See Stitch-and-Flip Square-in-a-Squares (page 11). Repeat to make 12 units.

3. Sew an F rectangle to the bottom edge of a unit from Step 2. Repeat with all 12 units.

4. Arrange the units from Steps 1 and 3, along with a B square, in 3 rows, as shown. Sew the units into rows, and then join the rows together. Repeat to make 3 blocks.

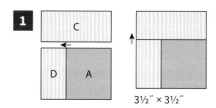

3½″ × 3½″

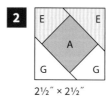

2½″ × 2½″

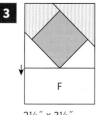

2½″ × 3½″

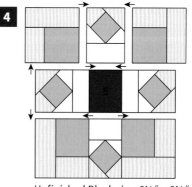

Unfinished Block size: 8½″ × 8½″

BLOCK 13
STAR FLOWER

FINISHED BLOCK: 8″ × 8″

Materials & Cutting Instructions

Yields 3 blocks.

Fabrics		Yardage and Cutting List
	Cosmos Teal FABRIC 6	**Yardage:** 1 fat quarter **Cut:** A: 36—2½″ × 2½″ ☐
	Nightshade Grass FABRIC 10	**Yardage:** 1 fat eighth **Cut:** B: 3—4½″ × 4½″ ☐
	Sprigs Navy FABRIC 18	**Yardage:** 1 fat quarter **Cut:** C: 12—4½″ × 2½″ ▭ D: 12—2½″ × 2½″ ☐

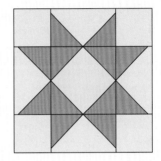

Piecing Instructions

Yields 3 blocks.

1. Sew 2 A squares to a C rectangle to make a flying geese unit. See Stitch-and-Flip Flying Geese (page 11). Repeat to make 12 units.

2. Use a B and 4 A squares to make a square-in-a-square unit. See Stitch-and-Flip Square-in-a-Squares (page 11). Repeat to make 3 units.

3. Arrange the units from Steps 1 and 2, along with 4 D squares, in 3 rows as shown. Sew the units into rows, and then join the rows together. Repeat to make 3 blocks.

1

A | A
C

4½″ × 2½″

2

A | A
B
A | A

4½″ × 4½″

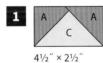

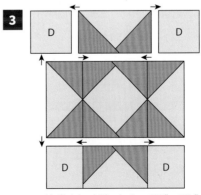

Unfinished Block size: 8½″ × 8½″

BLOCK 14
BELL FLOWER

FINISHED BLOCK: 8″ × 8″

Materials & Cutting Instructions

Yields 3 blocks.

Fabrics		Yardage and Cutting List
	Cosmos Aubergine FABRIC 13	Yardage: **1 fat eighth** Cut: A: 6—3″ × 3″ ☐ B: 12—2½″ × 2½″ ☐
	Nightshade Sangria FABRIC 14	Yaradge: 1 fat quarter Cut: C: 12—4½″ × 2½″ ▭
	Sprigs Sangria FABRIC 19	Yardage: 1 fat quarter Cut: D: 6—3″ × 3″ ☐ E: 24—2½″ × 2½″ ☐

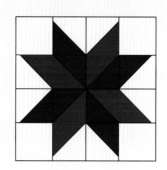

Piecing Instructions

Yields 3 blocks.

1. Use 6 pairs of A and D squares to make 12 half-square triangle units. See Two-at-a-Time Half-Square Triangles (page 13). Center and trim each unit to 2½″ × 2½″.

2. Sew an E square to the lower left corner of a C rectangle. See Stitch-and-Flip Corners (page 10). Sew a B square to the upper right corner the same way. Repeat to make 12 units.

3. Sew an E square to the left edge of a unit from Step 1 as shown. Then sew a unit from Step 2 to the bottom edge. Repeat to make 12 units.

4. Arrange 4 units from Step 3 in 2 rows as shown. Sew the units into rows, and then join the rows together. Press, spinning the center seam (see Spinning Seams, page 21). Repeat to make 3 blocks.

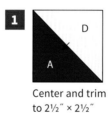

1

Center and trim to 2½″ × 2½″

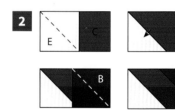

2

4½″ × 2½″

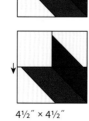

3

4½″ × 4½″

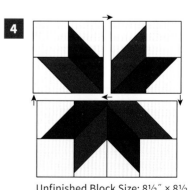

4

Unfinished Block Size: 8½″ × 8½″

BLOCK 15
TEA ROSE

FINISHED BLOCK: 4″ × 4″

Materials & Cutting Instructions

Yields 12 blocks: 6 dark and 6 light.

My sampler quilt uses dark and light variations of this block. The dark version uses Fabric 12 for pieces B and C and Fabric 13 for pieces D and E. The light version uses Fabric 14 for pieces B and C and Fabric 15 for pieces D and E.

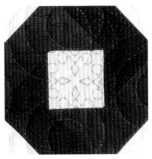

Light variation   Dark variation

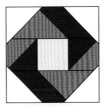

Light variation   Dark variation

Fabrics	Yardage and Cutting List
Filagree Buttercup FABRIC 11	Yardage: 1 fat eighth Cut: A: 12—2″ × 2″ ☐
Nightshade Aubergine FABRIC 12	Yardage: 1 fat quarter of each print From each fabric, cut: B: 12—3″ × 1¾″ ▭ C: 12—2″ × 1¾″ ▭
Nightshade Sangria FABRIC 14	
Cosmos Aubergine FABRIC 13	Yardage: 1 fat quarter of each print From each fabric, cut: D: 12—3¼″ × 1¾″ ▭ E: 12—1¾″ × 1¾″ ☐
Cosmos Sangria FABRIC 15	
Superior Solids White FABRIC 24	Yardage: 1 fat eighth Cut: F: 48—1½″ × 1½″ ☐

Piecing

Yields 12 blocks: 6 dark and 6 light. The dark version is shown in the piecing instructions.

1. Sew C rectangles to the left and right edges of an A square. Repeat to make 6 units.

2. Sew E squares to the upper left and lower right corners of a unit from Step 1. See Stitch-and-Flip Corners (page 10). Repeat with all 6 units.

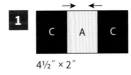

4½″ × 2″

4½″ × 2″

41

Block 15: Tea Rose

3. Paying careful attention to the angle of the pieces and seam line, join B and D rectangles. See Stitch-and-Flip Rectangles (page 12). Repeat to make 12 units.

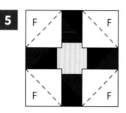 

4½″ × 1¾″

4. Join units from Step 3 to the top and bottom edges of a unit from Step 2 as shown. Repeat to make 6 units.

Unit size: 4½″ × 4½″

5. Sew F squares to the corners of each unit from Step 4. See Stitch-and-Flip Corners (page 10). Repeat to make 6 dark blocks.

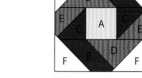

Unfinished Block Size:
4½″ × 4½″

6. Repeat Steps 1–5 with the light fabrics to make 6 light blocks.

Unfinished Block Size:
4½″ × 4½

BLOCK 16
FORGET-ME-NOTS
FINISHED BLOCK: 4″ × 4″

Materials & Cutting Instructions

Yields 4 blocks.

Fabrics		Yardage and Cutting List
	Nightshade Teal FABRIC 4	**Yardage:** 1 fat eighth **Cut:** A: 16—1⅞″ × 1⅞″ □
	Sprigs Sangria FABRIC 19	**Yardage:** 1 fat eighth **Cut:** B: 4—1⅞″ × 1⅞″ □
	Superior Solids White FABRIC 24	**Yardage:** 1 fat eighth **Cut:** C: 4—3½″ × 3½″ ⊠ D: 8—2″ × 2″ ◻

Piecing Instructions

Yields 4 blocks.

Arrange A and B squares with C and D triangles in diagonal rows as shown Sew the pieces into 3 rows. Sew the outer D triangles to the top left and bottom right rows. Then, join the rows together. Center and trim to 4½″ × 4½″. Repeat to make 4 blocks.

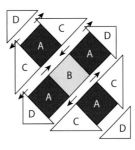
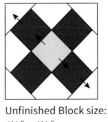

Unfinished Block size:
4½″ × 4½″

BLOCK 17
LEAFLETS

FINISHED BLOCK: 4″ × 4″

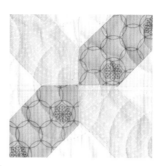 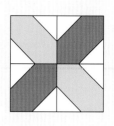

Materials & Cutting Instructions

Yields 10 blocks.

Fabrics		Yardage and Cutting List
	Cosmos Leaves FABRIC 9	Yardage: 1 fat eighth Cut: A: 20—2½″ × 2½″ □
	Nightshade Grass FABRIC 10	Yardage: 1 fat eighth Cut: B: 20—2½″ × 2½″ □
	Superior Solids White FABRIC 24	Yardage: 1 fat quarter Cut: C: 80—1½″ × 1½″ □

Piecing Instructions

Yields 10 blocks.

1. Sew 2 C squares to the upper right and lower left corners of an A square. See Stitch-and-Flip Corners (page 10). Repeat to make 20 units.

2. Sew 2 C squares to the upper right and lower left corners of a B square. See Stitch-and-Flip Corners (page 10). Repeat to make 20 units.

3. Arrange units from Steps 1–2 in 2 rows as shown. Sew the units into rows, then, join the rows together, and press, spinning the center seam (see Spinning Seams, page 21). Repeat to make 10 blocks.

2½″ × 2½″

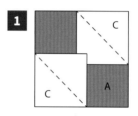 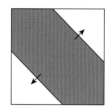

2½″ × 2½″

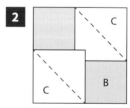 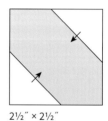

Unfinished Block Size: 4½″ × 4½″

BLOCK 18
SPRIGS

FINISHED BLOCK: 6″ × 4″

Materials & Cutting Instructions

Yields 4 blocks.

Fabrics		Yardage and Cutting List
	Stitches Moss FABRIC 8	**Yardage:** 1 fat eighth **Cut:** A: 16—2½″ × 2½″ ☐
	Cosmos Leaves FABRIC 9	**Yardage:** 1 fat eighth **Cut:** B: 8—2½″ × 2½″ ☐
	Superior Solids White FABRIC 24	**Yardage:** 1 fat eighth **Cut:** C: 48—1½″ × 1½″ ☐

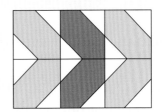

Piecing Instructions

Yields 4 blocks.

1. Sew 2 C squares to the upper right and lower left corners of an A square. See Stitch-and-Flip Corners (page 10). Repeat to make 16 units.

2. Sew 2 C squares to the upper right and lower left corners of a B square and press. See Stitch-and-Flip Corners (page 10). Repeat to make 8 units.

3. Arrange units from Steps 1–2 in 2 rows as shown. Sew the units into rows, then join the rows, pressing the middle seam open to reduce bulk. Repeat to make 4 blocks.

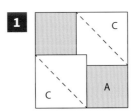
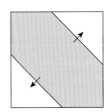

2½″ × 2½″

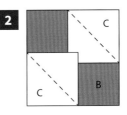
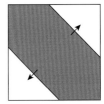

2½″ × 2½″

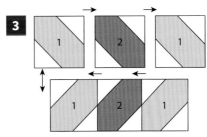

Unfinished Block Size: 6½″ × 4½″

45

Block 18: Sprigs

Additional Cutting Instructions

From Fabric 1, cut 10—2½″ × WOF fabric strips for binding.

> ### TIPS FOR SAMPLER ASSEMBLY
>
> • In general, press all seams open to reduce bulk. Some seams will want to lay open naturally while others will have a strong inclination to be pressed one way or the other, so listen to your quilt top and press seams in the way that works for you! When pressing seams open, take the time to back stitch at the beginning and end of each seam during the assembly process to prevent unraveling.
>
> • Some seams will nest … and some won't. Both are fine. Just do your best to match points and block edges.
>
> • Watch out for block seams folding over as you sew. Use plenty of pins and a stiletto or tailor's awl as you sew to avoid this as much as possible.
>
> • When rematching a point or fixing a folded-over seam, there is no need to rip out the whole row! Use your seam ripper to pop open a few stitches on either side of the problem area, then re-pin and re-sew that area.

Assembling Quadrants

Because the quilt top is made from blocks in a variety of sizes, it's impossible to sew the blocks together into rows and then join the rows. Instead, the quilt top is assembled in 4 quadrants. Then, the quadrants are joined together to finish the quilt top.

SECTION A

1. Gather:

- 3—Block 15
- 2—Block 18
- 1—Block 3, Block 4, Block 11, Block 12

Sew together the 3 Block 15s and 2 Block 18s in a row as shown in the middle of the diagram. Sew the Block 3 to the top edge.

Sew together Blocks 11 and 12 vertically. Then, sew a Block 4 to the left edge. Join the 2 units together.

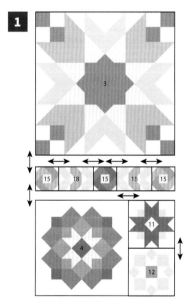

24½″ × 44½″

Completing the Flower Farm Sampler

2. Gather:

- 2—Block 15, Block 17

- 1—Block 6, Block 8, Block 11, Block 13, Block 14

Sew the 2 Block 15s and 2 Block 17s into a 4-patch formation as shown. Sew the Block 13 to the bottom edge. Then, sew the Block 8 to the right edge.

Sew together Blocks 11 and 14 vertically. Then, sew a Block 6 to the left edge. Join the 2 units together.

3. Join the units from Steps 1 and 2 as shown to make Section A.

24½″ × 32½″

24½″ × 76½″

SECTION B

1. Gather:

- 1—Block 2, Block 5, Block 12, Block 14

Join Blocks 12 and 14. Then, sew a Block 5 to the bottom edge. Finally, sew a Block 2 to the right edge.

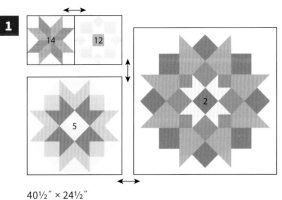

40½″ × 24½″

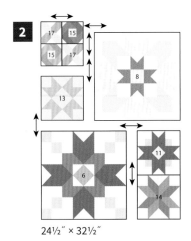

2. Gather:

- 2—Block 15, Block 17
- 1—Block 1, Block 8, Block 13

Sew the 2 Block 15s and 2 Block 17s into a 4-patch formation as shown. Sew the Block 13 to the left edge. Then, sew the Block 8 to the bottom edge. Finally, sew the Block 1 to the left edge.

3. Gather:

- 1—Block 6, Block 7, Block 9

Join Blocks 6, 7, and 9 into a vertical column.

4. Join the units from Steps 1–3 as shown to make Section B.

40½″ × 24½″

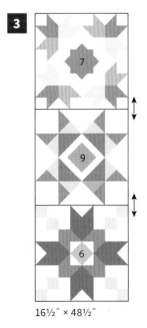

16½″ × 48½″

56½″ × 48½″

Completing the Flower Farm Sampler

SECTION C

1. Gather:

- 2—Block 16, Block 17

- 1—Block 9, Block 10, Block 12.

Sew together the 2 Block 16s and 2 Block 17s in a row as shown. Sew together Blocks 10 and 12. Arrange into 3 rows with Block 9, and sew the rows together.

2. Repeat Step 1, arranging the rows as shown, with:

- 2—Block 16, Block 17

- 1—Block 4, Block 10, Block 13

3. Gather:

- 3—Block 15

- 2—Block 18

- 1—Block 3

Sew together the 3 Block 15s and 2 Block 18s into a row as shown. Sew the Block 3 to the top edge.

4. Join the units from Steps 1–3 as shown to make Section C.

SECTION D

1. Gather:

- 2—Block 15, Block 17

- 1—Block 1, Block 7, Block 10

Join 2 Block 15s and 2 Block 17s into a 4-patch formation as shown. Sew a Block 10 to the left edge. Then, sew a Block 7 to the top edge. Finally, sew Block 1 to the left edge.

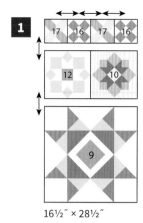

16½″ × 28½″

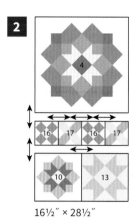

16½″ × 28½″

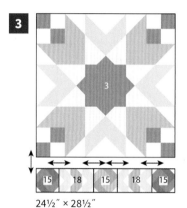

24½″ × 28½″

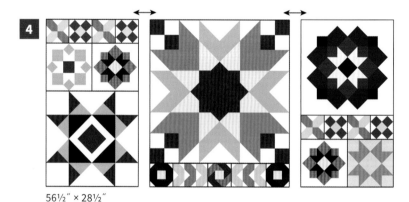

56½″ × 28½″

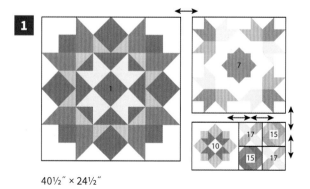

40½″ × 24½″

Flower Farm Sampler

2. Gather:

- 1—Block 2, Block 5, Block 11, Block 14

Join a Block 14 and a Block 11. Then, sew a Block 5 to the bottom edge. Finally, sew a Block 2 to the right edge.

3. Join the units from Steps 1 and 2 to make Section D.

Assembling the Quilt Top

Join Sections B and C. Then, sew Section A to the left edge. Finally, sew Section D to the bottom edge.

FINISHING THE QUILT

1. Layer the quilt top, batting, and backing. Baste the layers together.

2. Hand or machine quilt the quilt sandwich. The quilt shown is machine quilted with an allover simple swirling design.

3. Use the 2½″-wide binding strips to make a double-fold binding. Attach the binding to the quilt.

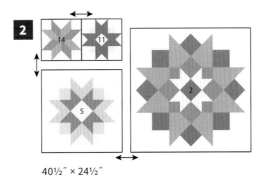

40½″ × 24½″

80½″ × 24½″

Quilt assembly, 80½″ × 100½″

MORE FANCIFUL QUILT PROJECTS

BRIGID'S GARDEN QUILT

Named for Brigid, the Celtic goddess of spring, *Brigid's Garden* is a celebration of the first blooms of spring! The corner squares in our Gentian Block (Block 6) come together to form a classic Irish Chain background, while our Dahlia Blocks (Block 5) create the illusion of flowers pushing their way up through the snow.

FINISHED QUILT: 78½″ × 78½″

**BLOCKS USED: BLOCK 5 (PAGE 26),
BLOCK 6 (PAGE 28)**

Before You Begin

One of my favorite ways of setting blocks within a quilt top is to surround my center, whole-versions of the blocks with a border of "half-drop" blocks … or blocks that are essentially cut in half (or quarters for the corner pieces).

For this quilt, you'll be assembling whole and half versions of Block 5, along with whole, half, and quarter versions of Block 6.

Unfortunately, making half and quarter versions of blocks isn't as simple as just cutting a finished block in half because you'll lose the necessary ¼″ seam allowance.

To simplify construction, we'll be joining the corner, side, and center units from each of the blocks together into "partial blocks" that we'll trim down to size before attaching the borders.

USE 108″-WIDE BACKING PRINTS AS BORDERS!

The hardest part about using a busy focal print as part of a border is the decision to either take the time to match up the pattern repeat (which can take loads of fabric and be tricky to get just right) or to settle for a mismatched print in the center of the quilt when the border units are seamed together.

Using a super-sized 108″-wide print intended as a quilt back is the perfect solution! You can cut the exact lengths you need AND showcase the beautiful pattern, uninterrupted!

Materials & Cutting Instructions

Yardage assumes 40″-wide fabric unless stated otherwise. For this quilt, the cut pieces are labeled with both a letter and a number. The number refers to the block number, while the letter still refers to the piece.

Fabrics	Yardage and Cutting List
Nightshade Aubergine	**Yardage:** 1 yard **For Block 5, cut:** 5A: 10—3″ × WOF strips; subcut into 128—3″ × 3″ □
Cosmos Aubergine	**Yardage:** 1¼ yards **For Block 5, cut:** 5B: 7—5½″ × WOF strips; subcut into 80—5½″ × 3″ ▭
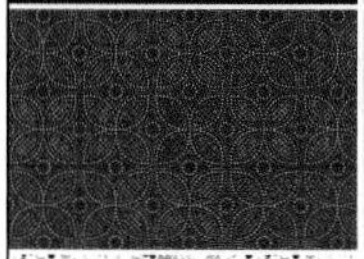 Nightshade Sangria	**Yardage:** ⅜ yard **For Block 5, cut:** 5C: 3—3″ × WOF strips; subcut into 32—3″ × 3″ □
 Sprigs Sangria	**Yardage:** 1½ yards **For Block 5, cut:** 5D: 2—5½″ × WOF strips; subcut into 12—5½″ × 5½″ □ 5E: 12—3″ × WOF strips; subcut into 144—3″ × 3″ □
Superior Solids White	**Yardage:** 2⅝ yards **For Block 5, cut:** 5F: 3—6″ × WOF strips; subcut into 32—6″ × 3½″ ▭ 5G: 1—5½″ × WOF strip; subcut into 40—5½″ × 1″ ▭ 5H: 3—3½″ × WOF strips; subcut into 32—3½″ × 3″ ▭ **For Block 6, cut:** 6E: 4—4½″ × WOF strips; subcut into 64—4½″ × 2½″ ▭ 6F: 13—2½″ × WOF strips; subcut into 196—2½″ × 2½″ □
Nightshade Navy	**Yardage:** 2¼ yards **For Block 6, cut:** 6A: 5—6½″ × WOF strips; subcut into 80—6½″ × 2½″ ▭ **For finishing the quilt, cut:** Borders and Binding: 16—2½″ × WOF strips
 Secret Garden Navy	**Yardage:** ⅝ yards **For Block 6, cut:** 6B: 7—2½″ × WOF strips; subcut into 112—2½″ × 2½″ □
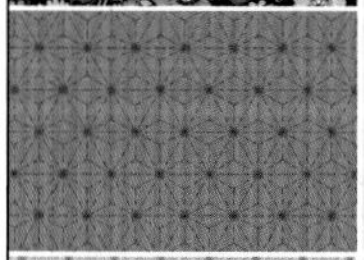 Stitches Teal	**Yardage:** ½ yard **For Block 6, cut:** 6C: 2—4½″ × WOF strips; subcut into 13—4½″ × 4½″ □
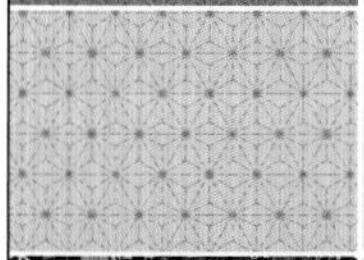 Stitches Moss	**Yardage:** ⅜ yard **For Block 6, cut:** 6D: 4—2½″ × WOF strips; subcut into 64—2½″ × 2½″ □
 Secret Garden Navy—108″-wide fabric	**108″-wide yardage:** ⅞ yard **For finishing the quilt, cut:** Borders: 4—5½″ × 108″ strips Note: 1⅜ yards 40″-wide yardage can be substituted if 108″-wide yardage is not available.

ADDITIONAL MATERIALS

- 87″ × 87″ square of batting
- 7¼ yards of 40″-wide fabric or 2½ yards of 108″-wide fabric for backing

Making the Blocks

All measurements include ¼″ seam allowances. Press after each seam. Pressing suggestions are indicated by the arrows in the assembly diagrams.

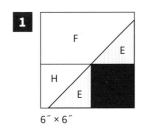
6″ × 6″

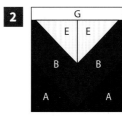
5½″ × 6″

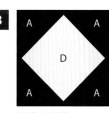
5½″ × 5½″

MAKING BLOCK 5

1. Using the C, E, F, and H pieces cut for Block 5, follow the instructions in Block 5: Dahlia, Piecing Instructions, Steps 1–3 (page 26) to make 32 units.

2. Using the A, B, E, and G pieces cut for Block 5, follow the instructions in Block 5: Dahlia, Piecing Instructions, Steps 4–6 (page 27) to make 40 units.

3. Using the A and D pieces cut for Block 5, follow the instructions in Block 5: Dahlia, Piecing Instructions, Step 7 (page 27) to make 12 square-in-a-square units.

4. Arrange the units from Steps 1–3 in 3 rows as shown. Sew the units into rows, and then join the rows together. Repeat to make 4 Block 5s.

5. Arrange the remaining units from Steps 1–3 in 2 rows as shown. Sew the units into rows, and then join the rows together. Repeat to make 8 "half" Block 5s.

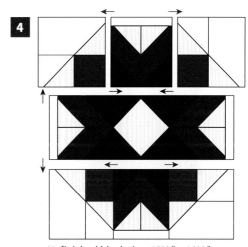
Unfinished block size: 16½″ × 16½″

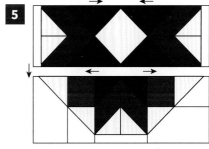
Unfinished block size: 16½″ × 11″

MAKING BLOCK 6

1. Using the B, D, E, and F pieces cut for Block 6, follow the instructions in Block 6: Gentian, Piecing Instructions, Step 1 (page 28) to make 32 units.

2. Using the A, B, and F pieces cut for Block 6, follow the instructions in Block 6: Gentian, Piecing Instructions, Steps 2–4 (pages 28–29) to make 40 units.

3. Using the C and F pieces cut for Block 6, follow the instructions in Block 6: Gentian, Piecing Instructions, Step 5 (page 29) to make 13 square-in-a-square units.

4. Arrange the units from Steps 1–3 in 3 rows as shown. Sew the units into rows, and then join the rows together. Repeat to make 5 Block 5s.

5. Arrange the units from Steps 1–3 in 2 rows as shown. Sew the units together into rows and then join the rows together. Repeat to make 4 "half" Block 6s.

6. Arrange the remaining units from Steps 1–3 in 2 rows as shown. Sew the units into rows, and then join the rows together. Repeat to make 4 "quarter" Block 6s.

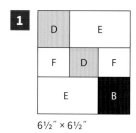

6½″ × 6½″

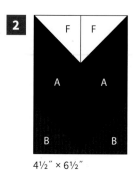

4½″ × 6½″

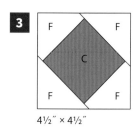

4½″ × 4½″

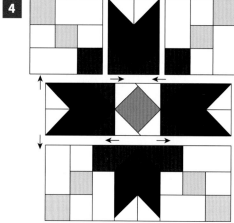
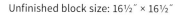
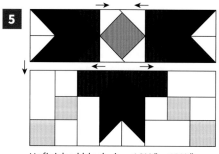

Unfinished block size: 16½″ × 16½″

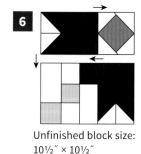

Unfinished block size: 16½″ × 10½″

Unfinished block size: 10½″ × 10½″

Assembling the Quilt Top

1. Referring to the quilt assembly diagram, arrange the full, half, and quarter blocks in 5 rows. Sew the units into rows and then join the rows.

> ### JAGGED QUILT EDGES!?!
> You'll notice that the edges of the half and quarter blocks won't line up around the perimeter of the quilt. They're not supposed to! The edges will be trimmed in the next step before attaching the borders.

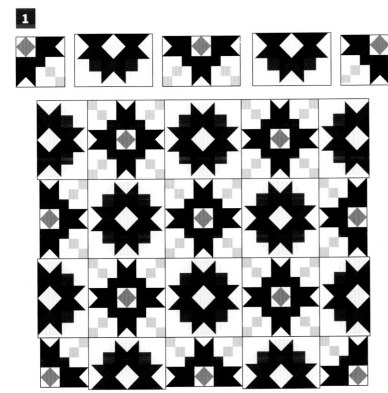

Quilt assembly

2. Trim and square up the quilt top, making sure to leave ¼″ beyond the star points on every block for seam allowance.

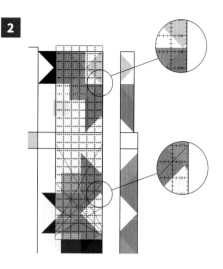

MEASURE THE QUILT TOP BEFORE CUTTING THE BORDERS

The border measurements in Steps 3–4 are exact mathematical measurements. Since all quilt tops can vary a little bit in actual constructed size, measure your own quilt top in several places, and make any needed adjustments to your own border sizes.

3. Join 7—2½″-wide Nightshade Navy border strips, end-to-end. From this pieced strip, cut 2—64½″ strips and 2—68½″ strips. Sew the shorter strips to the left and right edges of the quilt top. Sew the longer strips to the top and bottom edges.

4. From the 108″-wide Secret Garden Navy border strips, cut 2—68½″ strips and 2—78½″ strips. Sew the shorter strips to the left and right edges of the quilt top. Sew the longer strips to the top and bottom edges.

If using 40″-wide strips, sew the strips together end-to-end. From this pieced strip cut the border strips as directed in Step 4.

Quilt assembly

Finishing the Quilt

1. Layer the quilt top, batting, and backing. Baste the layers together.

2. Hand or machine quilt the quilt sandwich. The quilt shown is machine quilted with an allover orange peel lattice and floral design.

3. Use the 9 remaining Nightshade Navy 2½˝-wide binding strips to make a double-fold binding. Attach the binding to the quilt.

PRETTY MAIDS QUILT

I love how well the Block 8: Snapdragons and the Block 11: Morning Glory play together. We've used two similar colorways for the Snapdragon blocks to add some subtle visual interest. The negative space between the blocks creates a lovely sense of order, much like the English country gardens that inspired this quilt.

FINISHED QUILT: 76⅜″ × 76⅜″

BLOCKS USED: BLOCK 8 (PAGE 32), BLOCK 11(PAGE 37)

Materials & Cutting Instructions

The *Pretty Maids Quilt* uses two colorways of Block 8 (a medium version and a light version) along with a single version of Block 11. For this quilt, the cut pieces are labeled with both a letter and a number. The number refers to the block number, while the letter still refers to the piece. Yardage assumes 40″-wide fabric.

Fabrics		Yardage and Cutting List
	Color Weave Aqua	**Yardage:** ⅝ yard For the light variation of Block 8, cut: 8A: 5—3″ × WOF strips; subcut into 60—3″ × 3″ ▢
	Filagree Buttercup	**Yardage:** ¾ yard For Block 8, cut: 8B: 3—3½″ × WOF strips; subcut into 36—3½″ × 3″ ▭ 8C: 1—3″ × WOF strip; subcut into 9—3″ × 3″ ▢ For Block 11, cut: 11D: 5—1¾″ × WOF strips; subcut into 96—1¾″ × 1¾″ ▢

Continued on page 64.

Fabrics	Yardage and Cutting List
Nightshade Navy	**Yardage:** 1 yard **For the light variation of Block 8, cut:** 8D: 1—3″ × WOF strip; subcut into 20—3″ × 1¾″ ▭ 8E: 2—1¾″ × WOF strips; subcut into 40—1¾″ × 1¾″ ☐ **For finishing the quilt, cut:** Q: 1—2½″ × WOF strips; subcut into 12—2½″ × 2½″ ☐ Binding: 9—2½″ × WOF strips
Poinsettia Aqua	**Yardage:** ⅝ yards **For the light variation of Block 8, cut:** 8F: 2—4¾″ × WOF strips; subcut into 40—4¾″ × 1¾″ ▭ 8G: 4—1¾″ × WOF strips; subcut into 80—1¾″ × 1¾″ ☐
Sprigs Navy	**Yardage:** 1⅞ yard **For Block 8, cut:** 8H: 6—3″ × WOF strips; subcut into 72—3″ × 3″ ☐ **For Block 11, cut:** 11E: 5—3¼″ × WOF strips; subcut into 96—3¼″ × 2″ ▭ 11F: 5—2″ × WOF strips; subcut into 96—2″ × 1¾″ ▭ 11G: 9—1¾″ × WOF strips; subcut into 192—1¾″ × 1¾″ ☐
Superior Solids White	**Yardage:** 4¼ yards **For Block 8, cut:** 7—4¾″ × WOF strips; subcut into: 8I: 36—4¾″ × 2¼″ ▭ 8J: 72—4¾″ × 1¾″ ▭ 8K: 3—3″ × WOF strips; subcut into 36—3″ × 2¼″ ▭ 8L: 9—2¼″ × WOF strips; subcut into 144—2¼″ × 2¼″ ☐ **For the finishing the quilt, cut:** 3—16½″ × WOF strips; subcut into: M: 36—16½″ × 2½″ ▭ N: 2—12½″ × 12½″ ◨ O: 2—13″ × WOF strips; subcut into cut into 4—13″ × 13″ ⊠ P: 1—2½″ × WOF strip; subcut into 12—2½″ × 2½″ ☐
Filagree Aqua	**Yardage:** ½ yard **For the medium variation of Block 8, cut:** 8A: 4—3″ × WOF strips; subcut into 48—3″ × 3″ ☐
Poinsettia Navy	**Yardage:** ⅜ yard **For the medium variation of Block 8, cut:** 8D: 1—3″ × WOF strip; subcut into 16—3″ × 1¾″ ▭ 8E: 2—1¾″ × WOF strips; subcut into 32—1¾″ × 1¾″ ☐
Stitches Moss	**Yardage:** ⅜ yard **For Block 6, cut:** 6D: 4—2½″ × WOF strips; subcut into 64—2½″ × 2½″ ☐
Secret Garden Navy—108″-wide fabric	**108″-wide yardage:** ⅞ yard **For finishing the quilt, cut:** Borders: 4—5½″ × 108″ strips Note: 1⅜ yards 40″-wide yardage can be substituted if 108″-wide yardage is not available.

ADDITIONAL MATERIALS

- 85˝ × 85˝ square of batting

- 7⅛ yards of 40˝-wide fabric or 2⅜ yards of 108˝-wide fabric for backing

❋ ❋ ❋

Making the Blocks

All measurements include ¼˝ seam allowances. Press after each seam. Pressing suggestions are indicated by the arrows in the assembly diagrams.

1. Using the A–L pieces cut for the light version of Block 8, follow the Block 8: Snapdragons, Piecing Instructions (pages 32–33) to make 5 Block 8s.

2. Using the A–L pieces cut for Block 8 for the medium version of Block 8, follow all of the Block 8: Snapdragons, Piecing Instructions (pages 32–33) to make 4 blocks.

3. Using the A–G pieces cut for Block 11, follow all of the Block 11: Morning Glory, Piecing Instructions (page 37) to make 24 blocks.

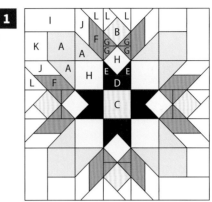

Unfinished block size: 16½˝ × 16½˝

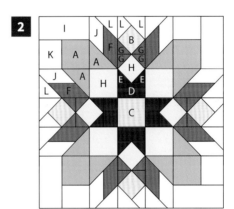

Unfinished block size: 16½˝ × 16½˝

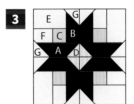

Unfinished block size: 8½˝ × 8½˝

Assembling the Quilt

1. Arrange 4 Block 11s as shown. Sew the blocks into rows, then join the rows together and press, spinning the center seams (see Spinning Seams, page 21). Repeat to make 4 units.

2. Sew an O triangle to the right edge of a Block 11. Then, sew an additional O triangle to the top edge. Repeat to make 8 units.

3. Referring to the quilt assembly diagram, arrange the units from Steps 1 and 2, the light and medium variations of Block 8, the M sashing rectangles, the P and Q cornerstones, and the N corner triangles in diagonal rows.

4. Join the M, Q pieces and P pieces into sashing rows, pressing the seams towards the M rectangles.

5. Join the blocks and the M rectangles into rows, pressing the seams toward the M rectangles.

6. Join the rows together, adding the N corner triangles last.

7. Trim and square the quilt top, making sure to leave ¼″ beyond the points of all the P cornerstone units for seam allowances. The quilt top should measure 76⅜″ × 76⅜″.

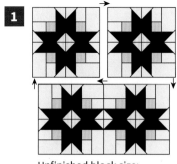

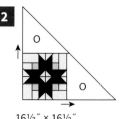

Unfinished block size:
16½″ × 16½″

16½″ × 16½″

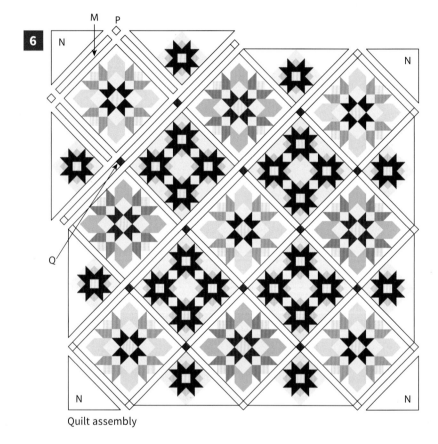

Quilt assembly

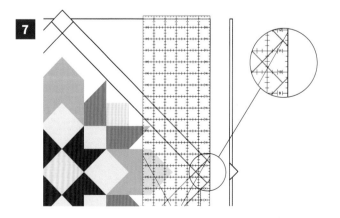

Finishing the Quilt

1. Layer the quilt top, batting, and backing. Baste the layers together.

2. Hand or machine quilt the quilt sandwich. The quilt shown is machine quilted with an allover looping diamond design.

3. Use the Nightshade Navy 2½˝-wide binding strips to make double-fold binding. Attach the binding to the quilt.

PRIMROSE QUILT

The simple addition of stitch-and-flip corners and a few flying geese units in the border units transform our Block 4: Primrose into this gorgeous, mosaic-inspired quilt!

FINISHED QUILT: 58½″ × 58½″

BLOCKS USED: BLOCK 4 (PAGE 24)

Materials & Cutting Instructions

The *Primrose Quilt* uses two colorways of Block 4: a dark version and a light version. Yardage assumes 40″-wide fabric.

Fabrics	Yardage and Cutting List
Nightshade Aubergine	**Yardage:** ⅞ yard **For the Dark variation, cut:** A: 1—4″ × WOF strip; subcut into 5—4″ × 4″ □ B: 2—2¼″ × WOF strips; subcut into 20—2¼″ × 2¼″ □ **For finishing the quilt, cut:** Binding: 7—2½″ × WOF strips
Cosmos Aubergine	**Yardage:** ⅝ yard **For the Dark variation, cut:** C: 4—4″ × WOF strips; subcut into 40—4″ × 4″ □

Continued on page 70.

Fabrics		Yardage and Cutting List
	Nightshade Sangria	Yardage: ⅞ yard For the Dark variation, cut: D: 2 4″ × WOF strips; subcut into 20 4″ × 2¼″ ▭ E: 4—2¼″ × WOF strips; subcut into 60—2¼″ × 2¼″ □ For the Light variation, cut: A: 1—4″ × WOF strip; subcut into 4—4″ × 4″ □ B: 1—2¼″ × WOF strip; subcut into 16—2¼″ × 2¼″ □
	Filagree Coral	Yardage: ⅝ yard For the Light variation, cut: C: 4—4″ × WOF strips; subcut into 32—4″ × 4″ □
	Sprigs Sangria	Yardage: ¾ yard For the Dark variation, cut: F: 4—2¼″ × WOF strips; subcut into 60—2¼″ × 2¼″ □ For the Light variation, cut: D: 1—4″ × WOF strip; subcut into 16—4″ × 2¼″ ▭ E: 3—2¼″ × WOF strips; subcut into 48—2¼″ × 2¼″ □
	Color Weave Lt. Rouge	Yardage: ⅜ yard For the Light variation, cut: F: 3—2¼″ × WOF strips; subcut into 48—2¼″ × 2¼″ □
	Filagree Cloud	Yardage: 2⅛ yards For both Dark and Light variations, cut: G: 2—7½″ × WOF strips; subcut into 36—7½″ × 1½″ ▭ H: 3—5″ × WOF strips; subcut into 36—5″ × 3¼″ ▭ I: 3—3¼″ × WOF strips; subcut into 36—3¼″ × 2¼″ ▭ J: 9—2¼″ × WOF strips; subcut into 144—2¼″ × 2¼″ □ For finishing the quilt, cut: K: 2—3½″ × WOF strips; subcut into 12—3½″ × 6½″ ▭
	Color Weave Lt. Grey	Yardage: 1½ yards For finishing the quilt, cut: L: 4—3½″ × WOF strips; subcut into 24—5½″ × 3½″ ▭ M: 6—3½″ × WOF strips; subcut into 64—3½″ × 3½″ □ Borders: 6—2½″ × WOF strips

ADDITIONAL MATERIALS

- 67″ × 67″ square of batting

- 3¾ yards of 40″-wide fabric or 2⅛ yards of 108″-wide fabric for backing

Making the Blocks

All measurements include ¼″ seam allowances. Press after each seam. Pressing suggestions are indicated by the arrows in the assembly diagrams.

1. Using the A–J pieces cut for the dark version of Block 4, follow the Block 4: Primrose, Piecing Instructions (pages 24–25) to make 5 blocks.

2. Using the A–J pieces cut for the light version of Block 4, follow the Block 4: Primrose, Piecing Instructions (pages 24–25) to make 4 blocks.

3. Sew M squares to each corner of each block from Steps 1 and 2. See Stitch-and-Flip Corners (page 10). Repeat with all 9 units.

1

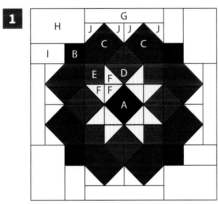

Unfinished block size: 16½″ × 16½″

2

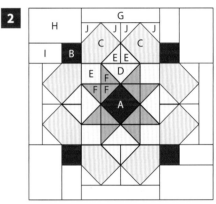

Unfinished block size: 16½″ × 16½″

3

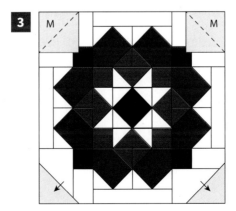

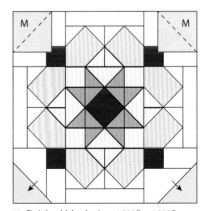

Unfinished block size: 16½″ × 16½″.

Making the Border Units

1. Use K and M pieces to make 12 flying geese units. See Stitch-and-Flip Flying Geese (page 11).

2. Sew L rectangles to the left and right edges of a flying geese unit from Step 1. Repeat to make 12 border units.

Assembling the Quilt

1. Referring to the quilt assembly diagram, arrange the blocks, border units, and the 4 remaining M squares in 5 rows as shown. Sew all the units into rows, and then join the rows together. Press all seams open to reduce bulk. The quilt top should measure 54½″ × 54½″.

> ### MEASURE THE QUILT TOP BEFORE CUTTING THE BORDERS
>
> The border measurements in Step 2 are exact mathematical measurements. Since all quilt tops can vary a little bit in actual constructed size, measure your own quilt top in several places, and make any needed adjustments to your own border sizes.

2. Join the Color Weave Lt. Grey 2½″-wide border strips end-to-end. From this pieced strip, cut 2—54½″ strips and 2—58½″ strips. Sew the shorter strips to the left and right edges of the quilt top. Sew the longer strips to the top and bottom edges. Press all seam allowances towards the border.

16½″ × 3½″

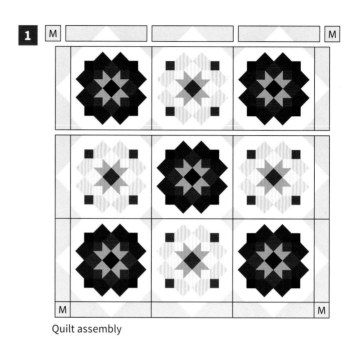

Quilt assembly

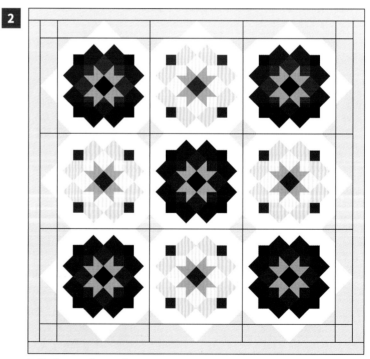

Quilt Size: 58½″ × 58½″

Finishing the Quilt

1. Layer the quilt top, batting, and backing. Baste the layers together.

2. Hand or machine quilt the quilt sandwich. The quilt shown is machine quilted with an allover swirling flower design.

3. Use the Nightshade Aubergine 2½″-wide binding strips to make a double-fold binding. Attach the binding to the quilt.

TULIP FARM QUILT

Just like with the *Primrose Quilt* (page 68), adding simple stitch-and-flip corners to the Block 7: Orchids not only transforms the blocks into cheery rows of tulips, but also creates gorgeous, starry secondary patterns as the blocks come together.

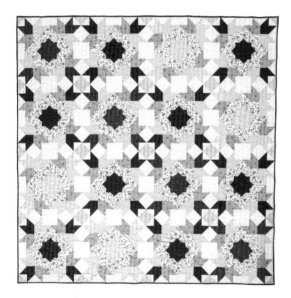

FINISHED QUILT: 64½″ × 64½″

BLOCKS USED: BLOCK 7 (PAGE 30)

Materials & Cutting Instructions

The *Tulip Farm Quilt* uses four different variations of the Block 7: Orchids. Each variation uses a different print for the flower petals and the center star (pieces A–D) but uses the same prints for the leaves and backgrounds (pieces E–M).

Fabrics	Yardage and Cutting List • Yardage assumes 40″-wide fabric.
Cosmos Leaves	**Yardage:** 1 yard **For all Block Variations, cut:** E: 4—4½″ × WOF strips; subcut into 64—4½″ × 2½″ ▭ F: 4—2½″ × WOF strips; subcut into 64—2½″ × 2½″ ▢
Nightshade Grass	**Yardage:** 1 yard **For all Block Variations, cut:** G: 4—4½″ × WOF strips; subcut into 64—4½″ × 2½″ ▭ H: 4—2½″ × WOF strips; subcut into 64—2½″ × 2½″ ▢
Cosmos Aubergine	**Yardage:** 1⅛ yard **For Block Variation 1, cut:** A: 1—4½″ × WOF strip; subcut into 4—4½″ × 4½″ ▢ B: 1—4½″ × WOF strip; subcut into 16—4½″ × 2½″ ▭ C: 1—3″ × WOF strip; subcut into 8—3″ × 3″ ▢ D: 2—1½″ × WOF strips; subcut into 32—1½″ × 1½″ ▢ **For finishing the quilt, cut:** Binding: 7—2½″ × WOF strips

Continued on page 76.

Fabrics	Yardage and Cutting List • Yardage assumes 40″-wide fabric.
 Nightshade Sangria	**Yardage:** ⅝ yard **For Block Variation 2, cut:** A: 1—4½″ × WOF strip; subcut into 4—4½″ × 4½″ □ B: 1—4½″ × WOF strip; subcut into 16—4½″ × 2½″ ▭ C: 1—3″ × WOF strip; subcut into 8—3″ × 3″ □ D: 2—1½″ × WOF strips; subcut into 32—1½″ × 1½″ □
Filagree Coral	**Yardage:** ⅝ yard **For Block Variation 3, cut:** A: 1—4½″ × WOF strip; subcut into 4—4½″ × 4½″ □ B: 1—4½″ × WOF strip; subcut into 16—4½″ × 2½″ ▭ C: 1—3″ × WOF strip; subcut into 8—3″ × 3″ □ D: 2—1½″ × WOF strips; subcut into 32—1½″ × 1½″ □
Stitches Mulberry	**Yardage:** ⅝ yard **For Block Variation 4, cut:** A: 1—4½″ × WOF strip; subcut into 4—4½″ × 4½″ □ B: 1—4½″ × WOF strip; subcut into 16—4½″ × 2½″ ▭ C: 1—3″ × WOF strip; subcut into 8—3″ × 3″ □ D: 2—1½″ × WOF strips; subcut into 32—1½″ × 1½″ □
 Sprigs Sangria	**Yardage:** 1½ yards **For all Block Variations, cut:** I: 8—4½″ × WOF strips; subcut into 128—4½″ × 2½″ ▭ J: 4—2½″ × WOF strips; subcut into 64—2½″ × 2½″ □
Superior Solids White	**Yardage:** 2⅛ yards **For all Block Variations, cut:** K: 4—4½″ × WOF strips; subcut into 64—4½″ × 2½″ ▭ L: 3—3″ × WOF strips; subcut into 32—3″ × 3″ □ M: 16—2½″ × WOF strips; subcut into 256—2½″ × 2½″ □
Color Weave Lt. Rouge	**Yardage:** ⅜ yard **For all Block Variations, cut:** N: 4—2½″ × WOF strips; subcut into 64—2½″ × 2½″ □

ADDITIONAL MATERIALS

- 73″ × 73″ square of batting
- 4⅛ yards of 40″-wide fabric or 2⅛ yards of 108″-wide for backing

Making the Blocks

All measurements include ¼″ seam allowances. Press after each seam. Pressing suggestions are indicated by the arrows in the assembly diagrams.

1. Using the A–D pieces cut for Block 7, Variation 1, along with E–M pieces, follow the Block 7: Orchids, Piecing Instructions (pages 30–31) to make 4 blocks (variation 1).

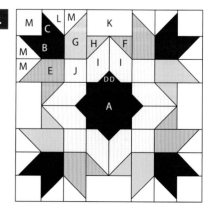

Unfinished block size: 16½″ × 16½″

2. Repeat Step 1 to make 12 additional Block 7s:
4 Block 7s using the pieces A–D cut for Variation 2,
4 Block 7s using the pieces A–D cut for Variation 3, and
4 Block 7s using the pieces A–D cut for Variation 4.

3. Sew N squares to each corner of each block from Steps 1 and 2. See Stitch-and-Flip Corners (page 10). Repeat with all 16 blocks.

Assembling the Quilt Top

Referring to the quilt assembly diagram, arrange the blocks into 4 rows. Sew the blocks in rows, and then join the rows together. Seams can be pressed open or in alternating directions, as desired. The quilt top should measure 64½″ × 64½″.

Finishing the Quilt

1. Layer the quilt top, batting, and backing. Baste the layers together.

2. Hand or machine quilt the quilt sandwich. The quilt shown is machine quilted with an allover floral design.

3. Use the Cosmos Aubergine 2½″-wide binding strips to make a double-fold binding. Attach the binding to the quilt.

Make 16 blocks, 4 in each colorway

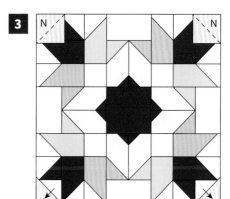

Unfinished block size: 16½″ × 16½″

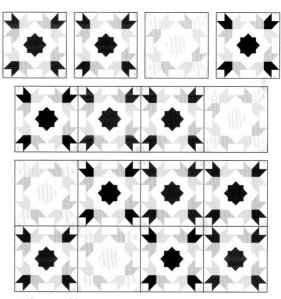

Quilt assembly

CLIMBING ROSES MINI QUILT

It may seem silly for the simplest quilts to be placed at the end of the book, but if you've worked your way through several of the previous projects, then chances are you have some leftover scraps just waiting for their chance to show off.

Both this quilt and the Among the Wildflowers Table Runner (page 84) are fantastic opportunities to turn some of our tiniest blocks into sweet little projects with a scrappy, patchwork feel.

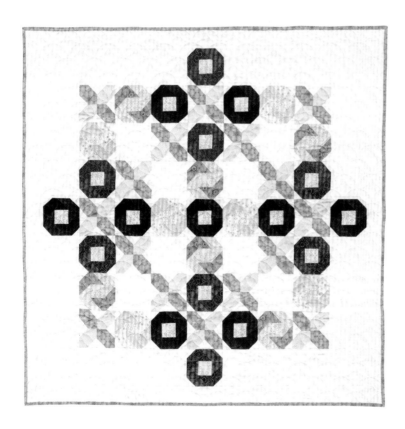

FINISHED QUILT: 40½″ × 40½″

BLOCKS USED: BLOCK 15 (PAGE 41), BLOCK 17 (PAGE 44)

Materials & Cutting Instructions

The *Climbing Roses Mini Quilt* uses four different colorways of the Block 15: Tea Rose, two light, along with one medium and one dark. Feel free to mix in as many different prints as you'd like!

For this quilt, the cut pieces are labeled with both a letter and a number. The number refers to the block number, while the letter still refers to the piece. Yardage assumes 40″-wide fabric. Fat quarters assume 18″ × 20″.

Fabrics	Yardage and Cutting List
Assorted Light Pink Prints	**Total Yardage:** ¾ yard For Block 15, cut 12 matching sets of: 15B: 2—3″ × 1¾″ ▭ 15C: 2—2″ × 1¾″ ▭ For Block 15, cut 12 matching sets of: 15D: 2—3¼″ × 1¾″ ▭ 15E: 2—1¾″ × 1¾″ □
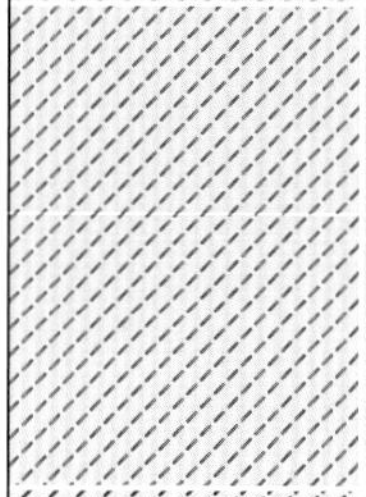 Assorted Medium Pink Prints	**Total Yardage:** ⅜ yard For Block 15, cut 8 matching sets of: 15B: 2—3″ × 1¾″ ▭ 15C: 2—2″ × 1¾″ ▭ For Block 15, cut 8 matching sets of: 15D: 2—3¼″ × 1¾″ ▭ 15E: 2—1¾″ × 1¾″ □
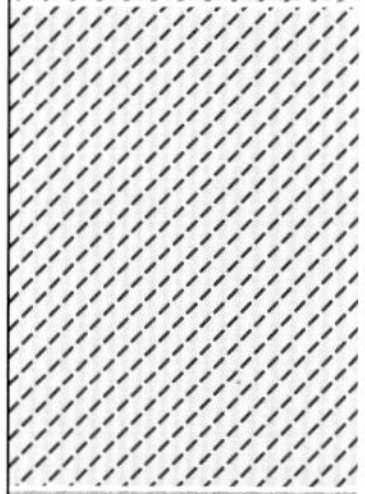 Assorted Dark Plum Prints	**Total Yardage:** ⅜ yard For Block 15, cut 9 matching sets of: 15B: 2—3″ × 1¾″ ▭ 15C: 2—2″ × 1¾″ ▭ For Block 15, cut 9 matching sets of: 15D: 2—3¼″ × 1¾″ ▭ 15E: 2—1¾″ × 1¾″ □
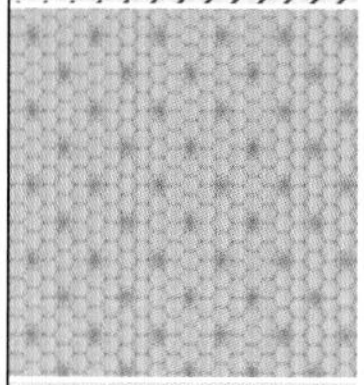 Cosmos Leaves	**Yardage:** ⅝ yard For Block 17, cut: 17A: 2—2½″ × WOF strips; subcut into 32—2½″ × 2½″ □ For finishing the quilt, cut: Binding: 5—2½″ × WOF strips
Nightshade Grass	**Yardage:** 1 fat quarter For Block 17, cut: 17B: 4—2½″ × 20″ strips; subcut into 32—2½″ × 2½″ □
Filagree Buttercup	**Yardage:** 1 fat quarter For Block 15, cut: 15A: 4—2″ × 20″ strips; subcut into 29—2″ × 2″ □

Superior Solids White	**Yardage:** 1½ yards
	
	For Block 15, cut:
	 15F: 5—1½″ × WOF strips; subcut into 116—1½″ × 1½″ □
	
	For Block 17, cut:
	 17C: 5—1½″ × WOF strips; subcut into 128—1½″ × 1½″ □
	
	For finishing the quilt, cut:
	 4—4½″ × WOF strips; subcut into:
	  A: 4—4½″ × 16½″ ▭
	  B: 4—4½″ × 12½″ ▭
	  C: 8—4½″ × 4½″ □
	 Border: 4—2½″ × WOF strips

ADDITIONAL MATERIALS

- 49″ × 49″ square of batting
- 2¾ yards of fabric for backing

Making the Blocks

All measurements include ¼″ seam allowances. Press after each seam. Pressing suggestions are indicated by the arrows in the assembly diagrams.

1. Using the A–F pieces cut for Block 15, follow the Block 15: Tea Rose, Piecing Instructions (pages 41–42) to make 29 blocks. If you're following the color scheme we suggested in the fabric requirements, you should make 12 blocks with the light pink prints, 8 blocks with the medium pink prints, and 9 blocks with the dark plum prints. Each block should use the same fabric for pieces B and C, and a second print for pieces D and E.

2. Using the A–C pieces for Block 17, follow the Block 17: Leaflets, Piecing Instructions (page 44) to make 16 blocks.

Block 15, unfinished size: 4½″ × 4½″

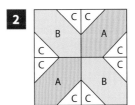

Block 17, unfinished size: 4½″ × 4½″

Assembling the Quilt Top

1. Arrange the Block 15s, Block 17s, and C squares in 7 rows, as shown. Sew the units into rows, and then sew the rows together. Seams can be pressed open or in alternating direction as desired.

2. Sew B rectangles to the left and right edges of a medium-toned Block 15. Repeat to make a second unit, then, join these units to the left and right sides of the quilt top.

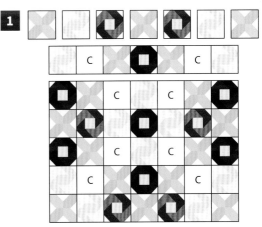

Quilt assembly part 1

3. Sew A rectangles to the left and right edges of a dark-toned Block 15. Repeat to make a second unit, then join these units to the top and bottom edges of the quilt top.

4. Trim 2 of the white 2½″ border strips to 36½″ long and join them to the left and right edges of the quilt top. Set aside the trimmed-off pieces for Step 5 (if needed).

5. If the border strips can accommodate the length, trim 2 of the remaining border strips to 40½″ long, and join these strips to the top and bottom edges.

If the border strips cannot accommodate 40½″ pieces, then join the remaining 2 border strips end-to-end plus a trimmed piece from Step 4. Cut 2 strips 40½″ to attach to the top and bottom edges from the new length.

6. Press all seam allowances towards the borders. The quilt top should measure 40½″ × 40½″.

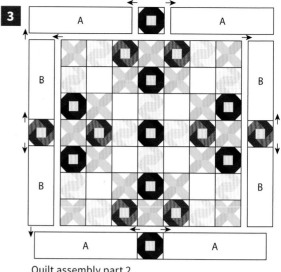

Quilt assembly part 2

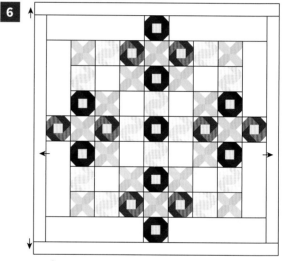

Border assembly

Finishing the Quilt

1. Layer the quilt top, batting, and backing. Baste the layers together.

2. Hand or machine quilt the quilt sandwich. The quilt shown is machine quilted with an allover classic orange peel design.

3. Use the Cosmos Leaves 2½˝-wide binding strips to make a double-fold binding. Attach the binding to the quilt.

AMONG THE WILDFLOWERS TABLE RUNNER

Every so often, one of our favorite hiking trails along the South Fork of the American River simply explodes in a super bloom of wildflowers, with lupines and greenery as far as the eye can see. Have fun repurposing some of your scraps from our earlier quilts and mix in as many prints as you'd like to create your own super blooming runner!

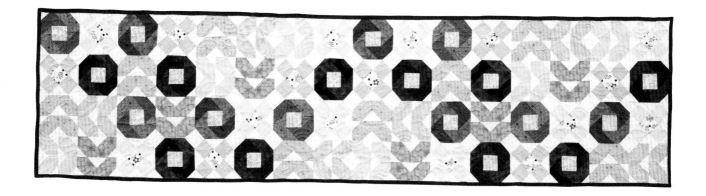

FINISHED RUNNER: 64½″ × 16½″

BLOCKS USED: BLOCK 15 (PAGE 41), BLOCK 16 (PAGE 43), AND BLOCK 18 (PAGE 45)

Materials & Cutting Instructions

For this runner, the cut pieces are labeled with both a letter and a number. The number refers to the block number, while the letter still refers to the piece. Yardage assumes 40″-wide fabric. Fat eighths assume 9″ × 20″.

Fabrics	Yardage and Cutting List

Assorted Navy Prints	**Total Yardage:** ⅜ yard
	For Block 15, cut 10 matching sets of:
	  15B: 2—3″ × 1¾″ ▭
	  15C: 2—2″ × 1¾″ ▭
	For Block 15, cut 10 matching sets of:
	  15D: 2—3¼″ × 1¾″ ▭
	  15E: 2—1¾″ × 1¾″ ☐

Assorted Teal Prints	**Total Yardage:** ⅜ yard
	For Block 15, cut 10 matching sets of:
	  15B: 2—3″ × 1¾″ ▭
	  15C: 2—2″ × 1¾″ ▭
	For Block 15, cut 10 matching sets of:
	  15D: 2—3¼″ × 1¾″ ▭
	  15E: 2—1¾″ × 1¾″ ☐

Assorted Aqua Prints	**Total Yardage:** ⅜ yard For Block 16, cut 18 matching sets of: 16A: 4—1⅞″ × 1⅞″ ☐
Assorted Green Prints	**Total Yardage:** ½ yard For Block 18, cut 26 matching sets of: 18A: 4—2½″ × 2½″ ☐
Nightshade Navy	**Yardage:** ½ yard For finishing the quilt, cut: Binding: 5—2½″ × WOF strips
Filagree Buttercup	**Yardage:** 1 fat eighth For Block 15, cut: 15A: 2—2″ × 20″ strips; subcut into 20—2″ × 2″ ☐
Sprigs Navy	**Yadage:** 1 fat eighth For Block 16, cut: 16B: 2—1⅞″ × 20″ strips; subcut into 18—1⅞″ × 1⅞″ ☐

Superior Solids White	**Yardage:** 1 yard
	For Block 15, cut:
	  15F: 4—1½″ × WOF strips; subcut into 80—1½″ × 1½″ ☐
	For Block 16, cut:
	  16C: 2—3½″ × WOF strips; subcut into 18—3½″ × 3½″ ⊠
	  16D: 2—2″ × WOF strips; subcut into 36—2″ × 2″ ◩
	For Block 18, cut:
	  18C: 8—1½″ × WOF strips; subcut into 208—1½″ × 1½″ ☐

ADDITIONAL MATERIALS

- 73″ × 25″ rectangle of batting
- 1⅜ yards of fabric for backing

Making the Blocks

All measurements include ¼″-wide seam allowances. Press after each seam. Pressing suggestions are indicated by the arrows in the assembly diagrams.

1. Using the A–F pieces cut from the assorted navy prints for Block 15, follow the Block 15: Tea Rose, Piecing Instructions (pages 41–42) to make 10 blocks. Repeat to make 10 additional Block 15s using the assorted teal prints. Each block should use the same fabric for pieces B and C, and a second print for pieces D and E.

2. Using the A–D pieces cut for Block 16 and the Block 16: Forget-Me-Nots, Piecing Instructions (page 43), make 18 blocks. Each block should use the same fabric for piece A.

3. Using the A and C pieces cut for Block 18: Sprigs, sew C squares to opposite corners of an A square. See Stitch-and-Flip Corners (page 10). Repeat to make 104 units.

4. Arrange 4 matching units from Step 3 in a 4-patch formation. Sew the units into rows, and then join the rows as shown. Press, spinning the center seam (see Spinning Seams, page 21). Repeat to make 26 units.

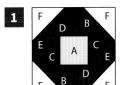

Block 15, unfinished size: 4½″ × 4½″

Block 16, unfinished size: 4½″ × 4½″

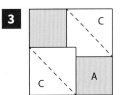

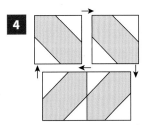

2½″ × 2½″

Block 18 (modified), unfinished size: 4½″ × 4½″

Assembling the Table Runner Top

1. Referring to the table runner assembly diagram, arrange the blocks into 4 rows. Sew the blocks into rows, and then join the rows together. Seams can be pressed open or in alternating directions, as desired. The runner top should measure 64½″ × 16½″.

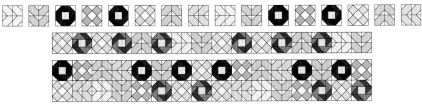

Table runner assembly

Finishing the Table Runner

1. Layer the runner top, batting, and backing. Baste the layers together.

2. Hand or machine quilt the quilt sandwich. The runner shown is machine quilted with an allover modern floral design.

3. Use the Nightshade Navy 2½″-wide strips to make a double-fold binding. Attach the binding to the quilt.

Photo by Shelley Cavanna

87

Among the Wildflowers Table Runner

ABOUT THE AUTHOR

Best-selling author Shelley Cavanna is a textile and quilt pattern designer and the owner of the Cora's Quilts pattern company. She makes her home near Sacramento, CA with her husband, their two sons, and their two dogs. From an obsession with modern, mosaic-inspired quilts, she makes it her mission to turn exquisite designs into approachable projects for quilters of all styles and skill levels, living up to her design mantra, "Stunning quilts made simple!"

When she's not in the studio, Shelley enjoys exploring the nearby Sierra Nevada mountains and practicing yoga. She is an avid reader of mysteries and historical fiction, a fan of audio books and true-crime podcasts, and a lover of squishy, cabley knitting projects!

Find out more about Shelley's patterns, classes, and quilting adventures at **CorasQuilts.com**

Photo by Leann Thompson, Leann Marie Photography

LET'S CONNECT!
JOIN OUR QUILTY COMMUNITIES!

One of my favorite things about being a quilter is our quilting community! I hope you'll stay in touch and share photos of your own Flower Farm Sampler projects with me. Here are a few ways we can keep in touch:

- Share your photos on Instagram using hashtags **#FlowerFarmSampler** and be sure to tag me **@CorasQuilts** so that I can find your projects too. Then, follow these hashtags to see more projects from quilty friends!

- Explore author-led quilt along and block-of-the-month programming, find video tutorials to walk you through techniques, and learn more about our Facebook quilt-along communities on our Flower Farm Sampler webpage at **CorasQuilts.com/flower-farm**